Petticoat Rebellion

THE ANNA PARNELL STORY

PATRICIA GROVES

THE ANNA PARNELL STORY

MERCIER PRESS
IRISH PUBLISHER – IRISH STORY

MERCIER PRESS

Cork

www.mercierpress.ie

Trade enquiries to CMD Booksource,
55a Spruce Avenue, Stillorgan Industrial Park,
Blackrock, County Dublin

ISBN: 978 1 85635 648 0

10 9 8 7 6 5 4 3 2 1

A CIP record for this title is available from the British Library

Printed and bound in the EU.

*To my family: Sarah and Kathryn, Alan and Theigie,
and my parents Eileen and Michael.*

Contents

Acknowledgements

I would like to thank the staff of the library at NUI Maynooth, particularly Marie Cullen, Susan Durack and Patricia Harkin who facilitated my research there.

This book would not have been possible without the support of The Parnell Society (www.parnellsociety.com), particularly Deirdre Larkin (Secretary) and Professor Donal McCartney, with a special thank you to Dr Pauric Travers (Chair) for his helpful feedback and for so kindly writing a foreword.

Warm wishes also to the team at Mercier Press, including Eoin Purcell, Clodagh Feehan, Mary Feehan and Wendy Logue. Thank you for guiding me through this process with your careful editing and attention to detail, while preserving the integrity of the text. Thank you for believing in the power of Anna's story.

And a personal thank you to my very patient friends in the Irish film industry, particularly Fiona Ashe, Shannon Moncrief and Mark Kelly.

Patricia Groves
Maynooth, May 2009

Foreword

Catherine Maria Anna Mercer Parnell (1852–1911) played an important role in the land agitation at a critical moment in its history; she was a pioneering feminist and leader of the Ladies' Land League; and she had an impact on the development of the wider nationalist movement. Yet, unlike her famous brother, Charles, she has been accorded at best a footnote in the pages of Irish history and only passing mention in history textbooks. Thankfully, in recent decades, particularly since the belated publication in 1986 of *The Tale of a Great Sham*, Anna Parnell's own account of the land agitation, this injustice has begun to be rectified. How and why she and her colleagues were written out of the national story is itself now a revealing part of the historical record. Patricia Groves' *Petticoat Rebellion* is a timely and welcome contribution to the rehabilitation of the reputation of Anna Parnell.

Enigmatic is a word commonly used about Charles Stewart Parnell, but it is even more apposite in the case of his patriot sister, Anna. Large gaps remain in our knowledge of her life and outlook. However significant advances have been made by historians whose research has been harvested and synthesised by Groves for a popular audience. Her eminently readable account is, as she puts it, a challenging story in which love, death, passion and politics are mixed in surprising ways.

Andrew Kettle, a land leaguer, who worked closely with both Anna and Charles Stewart Parnell, concluded that Anna had a better knowledge of the lights and shades of Irish peasant life, of the real economic conditions of the country, and of the social and political forces which had to be acted upon to work out the freedom of Ireland than any other person, man or woman, he had ever met. Kettle speculated that she would have worked the land revolution to a much better conclusion than her brother. Those who read *Petticoat Rebellion* will be better placed to evaluate the validity of this particular 'what if' in Irish history.

Dr Pauric Travers
Chair, Parnell Society

Extract of a message from President McAleese to the Parnell Society on the occasion of its visit to the grave of Anna Parnell, 5 April 2002

As a young woman, Anna Parnell became the leader and driving force in the organisation and spread of the Ladies Land League, ready to do battle for her ideals against all establishments – political, agrarian, patriarchal and ecclesiastical. This was the first movement to organise women for political objectives. Today we are fortunate that the range of opportunities open to women is greater than ever – in business, in politics, in sport, in community activities, in every sphere of public and private life. Anna Parnell would be proud of women today and she was justified when she said: 'When we are dead and gone and another generation grown up … they will point to us as having set a noble example to all the women of Ireland.' It is fitting that she be remembered for the significant contribution she made to the aspiration for, and the development of, a more just and caring community.

Mary McAleese
President of Ireland

Introduction

This book about Anna Parnell was inspired by a fingerprint in the dust of history – a small plaque high on the wall of the AIB Bank in O'Connell Street, Dublin, at the corner of Parnell Square. This small, circular plaque simply says 'Ladies Land League (1881–1882)'. I was intrigued.

Standing in an interminable queue in the bank in late 2006, I wrote 'Ladies Land League' on the back of an envelope and decided to find out more. I was curious for three reasons: firstly that someone considered that the organisation was important enough to merit a plaque on the wall, secondly that the Ladies' Land League existed for only two short years, and thirdly that throughout my time in the Irish education system I had never heard of them. There must have been a story behind that simple inscription.

Later that day, I began to research the Ladies' Land League, starting with the second Irish famine of the nineteenth century in the summer of 1879. It wasn't easy. Like panning for gold in a river bed, each sparkling fleck led to a small nugget of information: a name, a date, an event. And then the trail would go cold as Anna's name led inevitably to that of her very famous older brother, Charles Stewart Parnell, or his colleague Michael Davitt, or a reference to a text condemning her.

And then suddenly in 1882, like switching off a radio, there was a silence about Anna Parnell, and all references to the Ladies' Land League vanished. Usually, such a silence means that the subject has died, but Anna Parnell had lived a further twenty-nine years. But she hadn't lived her final decades in Ireland, the country she loved so much and for whose independence she had worked so hard. Surprisingly, Anna Parnell moved to England shortly after the Ladies' Land League was dissolved in 1882, and changed her name. Who, or what, was she distancing herself from? Was she in exile, or had she been banished, or was it possible that she had chosen to leave everything behind?

Why would the allegedly militant leader of an organisation portrayed as radical, decide to quietly leave the country and live in solitude in a small coastal town, under an assumed name? This didn't match the portrait of the extreme activist which Katharine O'Shea, Michael Davitt and others had painted. It was clear that a huge part of the story was missing. The only theory that made sense was if someone, or something, had silenced her. But who and why?

WHO WAS ANNA PARNELL?

Anna Parnell – younger sister of the talented statesman Charles Stewart Parnell – has been portrayed in Irish history as a militant activist who roamed the countryside creating havoc during the

Land War of the 1880s, and who had to be silenced for the good of Ireland. She was vilified and condemned in historical texts for over a century, and her one attempt to give her side of the story failed to find a publisher during her lifetime.

Anna Parnell was the leader of the Ladies' Land League, a charitable organisation set up to alleviate poverty and provide support to political prisoners following the Irish famine of 1879. The activities of the Ladies' Land League included bringing supplies to the poor in their hovels, preventing unfair evictions, buying food for prisoners and organising local groups of women to campaign for justice for the landless poor. There is no trace of any of the militant activism of which she is accused, only second-hand accounts written by people who had heard stories about her.

What made the Ladies' Land League so different from all the other groups fighting for Irish independence from the British – such as the Fenians, the Home Rulers and the gentlemen's Land League – was gender. As a woman, Anna somehow managed to establish a national network and mobilise women around the country in a way that had never been done before. Their work was very demanding physically – loading carts, travelling the unpaved country roads of Ireland and delivering provisions – and is all the more remarkable because this was during the late Victorian era when middle-class ladies wore impossibly tight corsets, billowing petticoats and restrictive shoes.

What makes this book more than just another retelling of the well-known story of the Irish Land War of 1879–1882 is how the relationship between Anna Parnell and her brother, Charles, sheds new light on those times. The perspective taken in this book is that of Anna Parnell herself – how did the Land War look from where she, and the women of Ireland, stood?

As children, Charles and Anna were reportedly very close, and as late as January 1881, when the Ladies' Land League was established in Dublin, they were working side by side with a common agenda for the future independence of Ireland. But in the midst of the political turmoil of the Irish Land War, Charles had a deep secret – his passionate love affair with Mrs Katharine O'Shea. While their affair blossomed, Anna's chances of ever marrying were destroyed by her lack of money, her general disdain for marriage and a public profile as an activist which ruined her reputation. The two women never got on, and Katharine, who knew Anna only through the sensational reports published in the British newspapers, considered Anna's behaviour shocking and considered her 'extreme'.

What was Charles' role in the silencing of his sister? Did he silence her at all, or did she simply decide not to talk about what happened? By the end of 1882, Anna and Charles' relationship had broken down so completely that it was widely, and incorrectly, reported that she refused to speak to her brother ever again. Anna herself wrote letters to the press contradicting this assumption, so annoyed was she by it.

To describe how she felt as she left Ireland in 1882, Anna wrote:

However long I might live, I knew that it would never again

be possible for me to believe that any body of Irishmen meant
a word of anything they said.

Anna Parnell, *The Tale of a Great Sham*

OUT-OF-PRINT TEXTS

Two key texts about Anna Parnell were published many years
ago, but are now out of print – Jane McL. Côté's excellent
biography of Anna Parnell and her elder sister Fanny, and
Anna's own account of the Ladies' Land League years, which
was finally published in book form in 1986, seventy-five years
after her death. Côté's work took four solid years of research,
and focuses in great detail on events in Ireland. It is an in-
depth academic work full of sound research, written by this
distinguished Canadian economist with family roots in
Roscommon, Kilkenny and Clare. It seems to be the nature of
the Parnell family that they attracted such interest from around
the world both in the nineteenth and twentieth centuries. They
were truly an international family. Luckily, a detailed search
of online bookstores turned up a solitary hardback copy, and I
ordered it immediately.

Anna's own book, *The Tale of a Great Sham*, was harder to track
down as it wasn't in the bookshops, or in any online bookshop.
Luckily, the National University of Ireland Maynooth had a copy
in its library, and I was able to obtain a reader's card and read it.
Hardly an accessible text! The original manuscript is also available
in the National Library. Anna's *Tale* is fascinating because it is an
in-depth analysis and a critique of political policies during the

Land War. The version published in 1986 was shorter than the 70,000 words Anna originally wrote, as it had been edited by Dana Hearne.

That Anna, a young woman, would have such an in-depth understanding of the politics of the time is surprising, especially since women at that time were not permitted to participate in politics, and were not even permitted to vote. It is clear that both she and her brother Charles must have spent some considerable time debating the politics of the day. It is also clear that she must have kept a diary, as was common with women of that era. She describes everything in such detail in her manuscript that either she had an exceptional memory, which is a possibility, or she had kept notes at the time. However, no trace of diaries kept by her have ever been found.

Côté's study is an excellent academic work, and Anna's own text is a strong political analysis and rejoinder to Michael Davitt's *Fall of Feudalism* which painted the Land War as a huge success.

Hearne and others, in critiquing Anna's *Tale*, usually state that a key flaw in the text is that Anna has completely removed all personalities from it. This is usually accompanied by a comment that Anna believed history should be about classes and events, and not about individuals. What surprised me as I read her *Tale* was that I did not find this entirely true. Her *Tale* is in fact full of names, dates, places, anecdotes and stories. Anna did not remove *all* personalities; she removed only the names of the leaders of the Land League, most significantly, her brother Charles.

In her *Tale*, the leadership is presented as being one body, with no individual head. From her perspective, this was probably true; deprived of the insider knowledge of the League's leadership, the leadership would have presented an inscrutable and impenetrable front to her and her Ladies. Perhaps it was an intentional reprimand to Michael Davitt for his text *Fall of Feudalism*, in which he was very specific about Anna; perhaps it was to avoid laying the blame for bad decision-making on any one person.

In any event, given Anna's previous written work, such as *Notes from the Ladies Cage*, and her reputation for getting straight to the point in as blunt and clear language as possible, her gentle blurring of who was ultimately to blame for the 'sham' of the title could in fact be interpreted as her own distinctive way of softening the blow of the text she felt compelled to write.

Perhaps it was one last, noble way of maintaining the dignity of her brother's memory.

However, we still know very little about Anna herself: she refused to publicise herself, and only one photograph of her is known to exist. She was a very private person who never explained herself to anyone. But this made me even more determined to find out about her.

Who was this extraordinary young woman who managed to cause so much controversy? How could a respectable young lady be perceived as a threat to both the Fenians and the Republicans? What was it that happened between her and her brother that so fatally damaged their relationship? Why did Archbishop McCabe of Dublin and Archbishop Croke of Cashel argue so ferociously over her that Bishop Moran of Ossory was forced to intervene? Why, despite this, did the argument continue until it was eventually resolved by Pope Leo XIII in Rome? This raging argument within the Catholic hierarchy was even more intriguing because Anna wasn't even Catholic – she was a member of the Church of Ireland.

Each thread of research led to another country, another controversy and another perspective on her character. But what was missing was any evidence of the alleged militant activities which were used to condemn her so thoroughly.

Anna learned about the value of public relations during her time fundraising in America in 1879. Back home in Ireland, she always made a point of inviting the local press to all of the events that she organised. The newspapers sent reporters, who printed her speeches verbatim. These speeches were then summarised by the regional papers. Not one of these reporters ever witnessed the alleged militant activity of which she was subsequently accused. How could all of these reporters have missed what would have been sensational front-page news? Or perhaps, as is more likely, she didn't actually do any of the things of which she was later accused.

There is evidence that Anna had a 'social justice' agenda, in common with many female activists of her time, such as Octavia Hill, a pioneer for social housing for the poor in London. Anna would most certainly have heard of Octavia's work, and would have been intrigued by her new method of managing quality housing for the poor in a way which also benefited the landlords.

In the nineteenth century, it was common for ladies of the upper classes to become involved in philanthropy to aid those in need. Indeed, it was as much a part of a young lady's life as embroidery or singing lessons. These women were often pioneers in campaigning for housing rights for the urban poor, sometimes setting up their own small charitable organisations. Housing was seen as a suitable endeavour for ladies; after all, it was a truth universally acknowledged that a woman's place was in the home.

Anna was also heavily influenced by her older sister, Fanny, who had written some militant poems in her teens. Fanny also wrote a pacifist poem which clearly stated the position of the Ladies' Land League at the time the Home Rulers called for 'Rent at the Point of the Bayonet':

> Hold your peace and hold your hands,
> not a finger on them lay, boys!
> Let the pike and rifle stand, we have found a better way, boys.

I wanted to discover more about this young woman, her family and the society in which she lived. The more I read, the more I realised she was a pioneer in so many ways – humanitarian aid, land reform and justice for the poor. Her passionate character simply couldn't accept the *laissez-faire* attitude of Victorian society: she had to get out there and do something to help those in need.

When she was appointed to take over the administrative work of the Land League while the male leaders were in prison, she had to decide herself what to do, and chose the familiar work of providing charitable relief to the poor and the evicted. And when her brother and the Land Leaguers were imprisoned, she provided food for them as well. Hardly militant activities.

Somehow, because she was so successful in her work, a mythology was built around her, and pundits of the day began to comment that the men of Ireland were hiding behind the ladies' petticoats. Indeed, the Ladies' Land League were referred to as 'Captain Moonlight in petticoats', and Anna, as an Irish Joan of Arc leading a battalion of *vierges de sang* (virgins of blood).[1] It was this dangerous legend, which undermined the credibility of the male leaders, that was probably instrumental in her downfall.

When reading biographies and histories of famous Irish women in the early twentieth century, the phrase 'and was a member of the Ladies' Land League' appears with surprising regularity. Women such as Jennie Wyse Power, Katharine Tynan and Helena Molony were clearly proud of their connection with the Ladies' Land League, or they would not have highlighted this experience in their diaries and memoirs, nor so clearly used their time in the League to indicate their suitability for future political involvement. But very little was said about what they did in the Ladies' Land League. It was as if they too had been sworn to a vow of silence.

Anna's story cannot be told by looking solely at the facts and events of Irish history. To do that leads back to the Land War and her brother, Charles Stewart Parnell. Her story only begins to make sense when the lens of history is instead focused outwards at the world, in the way that Anna and the Parnell family might have seen it. Most histories of the Land War in Ireland look inwards, examining domestic events and personalities under a microscope. However, the Parnell family were different to most Irish families of the time. The family was headed by John Parnell, a Protestant Anglo-Irish landowner, and his American wife Delia. Anna was an Anglo-Irish-American, with an international and cosmopolitan upbringing, and she was highly educated and well-read in a way that was extraordinary for a woman of her time. The entire Parnell family would therefore have seen the world in a different way to the majority of Irish people.

By taking this telescopic view of international affairs of the times, the Ladies' Land League was transformed into an organisation of international importance; with a fundraising office in New York, printing operations in Paris and London, influence in Rome, and conflict with Prime Minister William Gladstone and Queen Victoria.

The backlash against Anna by the establishment – and indeed both sides of the Land War – suddenly comes into sharp focus and a new picture emerges. She was not simply a talented organiser and advocate for the poor: her peaceful activism made her, and others of the Ladies' Land League, a threat to the entire *status quo* of Victorian society and the Irish Republican movement. But as women, they were untouchable under the law. The British government was quite simply too afraid to imprison them for fear of American retaliation or a popular civil uprising.

They were neither operating within the direct control of Charles Stewart Parnell and the male Land Leaguers, nor were they within the control of the lord lieutenant of Ireland or the British government. This made both the British government and the Irish republicans very uncomfortable. It also meant that the Ladies were in the curious situation of being able to operate totally unfettered, at a time when even suspicion of anti-landlord activity meant instant imprisonment without trial – as it had done for the leaders of the men's Land League. For the first time, Irish women suddenly had a taste of real freedom and independence.

AN AMERICAN HEROINE

Anna was a true American heroine, from an extraordinary family, who brought American pragmatism to bear on the 'Irish Question' and who took a fearless, hands-on approach to poverty and injustice.[2] Granddaughter of Rear Admiral Charles Stewart, who vanquished the British at sea in 1815, her American background served her well for fundraising and publicising the Irish cause. And she spoke directly to women in a way that was previously unheard of in Ireland.

The Parnell family were described in 1880 by journalist Timothy Healy, who was sent to New York to work as a personal secretary to Charles Stewart Parnell, as 'the most extraordinary family I ever came across. The mother, I think, is a little "off her nut" in some ways and, for that matter, so are the rest of them.'[3] To their contemporaries, perhaps the Parnell family's unique approach to politics and civil action did seem quite extreme by the restrained standards of Victorian England.

Anna was also the subject of a scathing criticism by Charles' future wife, Katharine, who wrote: 'the wild spirit of these Ladies was extreme; in Anna Parnell it was abnormal'. Katharine knew or suspected that Anna's high profile work posed a threat to her future husband's political career so it is hardly surprising that she was so outspoken. It was only natural that she would try to protect her husband. And when Anna discovered Charles' illicit affair with Katharine, she in turn was concerned that the affair could destroy his political career. Therefore, the animosity between these two women, who both loved the same man in different ways and who each saw the other as his nemesis, begins to make sense.

Meanwhile, on the other side of the Atlantic, America was still recovering from the aftermath of the American Civil War. It was the time when the so-called 'wild west' was being tamed. To the American public, the romantic image of Anna's army of brave young Ladies feeding the sick and the poor, her handsome elder brother Charles lobbying for political change, with their sister Fanny tirelessly fundraising in New York, the Parnell family must have seemed true American heroes.

The Parnell family's influence spanned the Atlantic; Fanny and Delia tapped into the Irish-American *zeitgeist* of the time, Anna challenged traditional views of the role of women, and Charles tested the legislative process in Britain to its limits. Never before, or since, has one family had so much influence in such a short time. Anna's story also resonates throughout

Europe and America, and in any country with a history of colonialism.

THE LIFE OF A LADY

Since her birth, Anna Parnell had enjoyed the benefits of a young Victorian lady's upbringing. She attended finishing school and enjoyed life as a debutante in London and Paris, attending balls, parties and musicals. She was a member of 'society', a contemporary of Oscar Wilde, and she associated with the type of people about whom he wrote with such humour. She was probably one of the 'American' ladies whom Oscar Wilde found so unfathomable.

From the beginning of the nineteenth century and throughout Queen Victoria's reign, it was considered the duty of every young lady to visit the poor. Mrs Beeton stated in her best-selling book, *The Art of Household Management*, published in 1861, that the mistress of a house must visit the poor in their own homes, to truly understand how they live, and to provide assistance where needed. Jane Austen, whose novels were published from 1811–1816, wrote about the regular visits of her various heroines to the cottages of the sick and the poor in their neighbourhoods.

Anna Parnell, and her mother and sisters, would have visited local families in distress, and were probably very familiar with the poverty of Irish peasants. They would have visited with small gifts of food, blankets or clothing, as was the custom of the day. The work of the Ladies' Land League was a natural extension of this, albeit better funded and much more organised. Anna's father spent time as a Poor Law Guardian and Justice of the Peace, and was a committed Christian.

'HISTORY' VERSUS 'SOCIAL HISTORY'

History, in its simplest form, is often just a list of names, a column of dates and a series of events. These include Land War highlights such as the Kilmainham Treaty, the shocking imprisonment without trial of the Land Leaguers, Home Rule and Prime Minister William Gladstone's Land Acts, all listed in children's schoolbooks on Irish history. These are the simple markers that schoolchildren learn, but they tell us nothing of the complex motivation of the characters, and the different ways in which they all worked for the same goal.

A more complex analysis of the past is called 'social history', which has many definitions, including history written from the point of view of the people rather than its leaders, or viewing historical events from the perspective of social trends. This book is written primarily as a social history.

Anna ultimately became the tragic heroine in the story of the Ladies' Land League. Even though her name, and that of the Ladies' Land League, appears like an occasional shadow in Irish historical footnotes, she is usually lost again in the text. History often points fingers at leading figures in a conflict to decide who was right and who was wrong. But the more I researched the Parnell family, the more I came to realise that both Anna and Charles were, in their own way, right about the Ladies' Land

League, and they both acted accordingly. And at the forefront of every decision was Irish freedom.

Anna and Charles were fighting for the same goal, but in different ways: Charles through the political process, Anna through direct action. Each tried to protect the other in the only way they knew how – by pointing out to each other the error of their ways, in the blunt and frank way that only brothers and sisters can. These loyal efforts to persuade the other they were wrong only served to make them more determined to maintain their own positions. These were the actions of a brother and sister who respected and admired each other, not of two antagonists locked in combat.

The truth of their special relationship becomes crystal clear when the years of 1879–1882 are carefully plotted in sequence. Not by noting the series of events, or by placing markers on a timeline, but by following their intimate story, moment by moment. Although Charles was always closer to Fanny, when Fanny remained behind in New York and he worked more closely with Anna, his relationship with her blossomed.

The 'Irish Question' was a riddle which even the most brilliant political minds of the time could not solve. Each character in the story – Anna, Charles, Queen Victoria, Michael Davitt, William Gladstone – believed themselves to be the main protagonist, and in many ways, they were. As the story progresses, the question of who is 'right' becomes harder to work out, and you, just like historians over a hundred years later, will have to make your own decision. It is a challenging story, in which love, death, passion and politics are mixed in surprising ways.

FROM HISTORICAL FOOTNOTE TO LEADING LADY

It has been said that history is always written by the victors, and this is certainly true in Anna Parnell's case. Although restricted by tight Victorian clothing, she led a petticoat rebellion across the Irish countryside, and it was these very petticoats, symbols of dainty femininity, which ultimately led to the destruction of the Ladies' Land League.

The Ladies' Land League was a benevolent organisation that existed for only a brief time – eighteen months – but was influential beyond anyone's expectations. It was born in the aftermath of the Great Irish Famine, which reduced the population from eight million in 1841 to six million in 1851, through starvation, disease, exposure and emigration. The remaining population lived under the constant threat of evictions and land-grabbing. Anna Parnell established the Ladies' Land League to do something about these injustices.

The Ladies' Land League was airbrushed out of history and until recently only glimpses of their story remained. In untangling the story of the Ladies' Land League by focusing on its Irish leader, Anna Parnell, I hope that more people will find out about this missing piece from Ireland's fascinating history. This book aims to write Anna Parnell and the Ladies' Land League back into popular history: the petticoat rebellion where respectable ladies fought the Land War with baskets of food and poetry, and refused to pay the 'Rent at the Point of the Bayonet', even though it meant their own downfall. *Petticoat Rebellion* has been written as a celebration of the life and times of this extraordinary young woman.

Jane McL. Côté, biographer of Fanny and Anna Parnell, said that upon the death of Anna Parnell in 1911, 'Ireland promptly forgot her'. The centenary of Anna's death is in 2011. Maybe this time170 , Ireland will not forget her.

I

A Birth in Turbulent Times

Catherine Maria Anna Mercer Parnell – later known affectionately as simply Anna – was born on the 13 May 1852, during one of the most turbulent periods in Irish history. This tiny infant, her American mother's tenth child, was destined to become one of Ireland's most notorious activists.

While this quiet, dark-haired baby slept, the world around her was changing rapidly, much to the delight of her five year old brother, Charles Stewart Parnell, who was fascinated by engineering and mechanical devices.

Anna's mother was Mrs Delia Parnell (née Stewart), who was the daughter of Commodore (later Rear Admiral) Charles Stewart. He was a celebrated American naval hero who had captured two British ships in February 1815 during the Anglo-American War and was even a candidate for the American presidency in 1838.

Delia revelled in society, the good life, and loved being the centre of attention. Before her marriage, she had enjoyed a life of international travel and parties, and she found life in the Irish country estate of Avondale to be far less exciting than London, Paris and New York. From the earliest days of her marriage, and like so many women of her day, her independence was swallowed up by a fertile marriage which produced a quick succession of children. Her first child, a son called William, was born the year after she married, but he died when only a few months old. She had eight more children before she gave birth to Anna.

Anna's father was John Parnell, a young Anglo-Irish gentleman, heir to the neo-classical country house and estate of Avondale, in the lush grasslands of County Wicklow. He was a cousin of Lady Powerscourt, whom he called 'Aunt Do' and was fiercely proud of his English roots. He always considered himself an Englishman. He was educated in Eton and Cambridge, and was conservative in his politics. Although many of his close relations were heavily involved in the deeply conservative Protestant Evangelical movement, he remained staunch Church of Ireland. He had a noted preference for austerity: meals were simple and the family's lifestyle was modest at the family home in Avondale.

Delia and John met and married in 1835 while he was in America, but they were not ideally suited. He had found life within the American city of Washington as dull as she would find life in the Irish countryside. They lived in Ireland for two years before returning to America with their new baby daughter. This baby was also called Delia, and she was born in 1837, the same year that the eighteen-year-old Queen Victoria ascended the throne of England.

They returned to Ireland after what John considered three interminable months, but after the births of their son Hayes in 1838 and daughter Emily in 1841, he found himself forced to return to Washington for another visit to the adoring grand-parents. In Washington, Delia found that she was pregnant yet again. The family returned home soon after, although by this stage Mrs Parnell was becoming fatigued by the constant child-bearing.

Unwilling to venture to America again, it was the turn of the children's grandmother to come to Ireland. She was not impressed with country life in Avondale, no doubt empathising with her exhausted daughter, and suggesting that a change of scene might be in order. Soon after, the ever-expanding young family moved for a time to the salty air of the English seaside village of Brighton, and the estate at Avondale was rented out to Lord Kildare.

This frequent travelling was characteristic of the Parnell family. The extended family were scattered and settled through-out Europe and America, and the Irish Parnells were never inclined to stay in one place for very long with the promise of adventure and hospitality across the seas. But the quiet, country estate of Avondale formed the anchor which gave the Irish Parnells a much-needed sense of permanence, and they frequently returned there.

Delia had eleven children in total: William, Delia and Hayes, Emily Letitia (1841), John Howard (1842), Sophia (1845), Charles Stewart (1846), Fanny Isabel (1848), Henry Tudor (1850), Catherine Anna Maria Mercer (1852) and finally Theodosia (1853).

Within a year of Theodosia's birth, their eldest surviving son, Hayes, then a young man of fifteen, died after a day's hunting at Avondale. Hayes had been out hunting with his father and during the hunt began to feel unwell. When he got home, he was sent to bed. His condition got progressively worse, and he was eventually diagnosed with pleurisy. He died shortly afterwards. Although the hunting itself was clearly not the cause of his death, Côte reports that John Parnell sold his horses and never went hunting again. Never comfortable with country life or its pursuits, Delia had always considered horse-riding to be a dangerous activity, and she blamed her husband for her son's death. This was the second son that Delia had lost and her grief was understandable. After seventeen years of bearing children regularly, at the age of thirty-six, Delia had no more children and the marriage was soured from that point onwards.

Anna was born two years after the end of the Irish potato famine of 1845–1850, a time which is still remembered in Ireland with simmering resentment for the way the crisis was handled.

From Ireland to Russia the nutritious potato, imported from the Americas, had quickly been adopted by European peasants living on poor soil. Even English and Scottish peasants adopted the food. Rich in carbohydrates and vitamins, potatoes enabled farmers and farm labourers to feed themselves from tiny plots of land, freeing up more of their land to grow cash crops such as grains.

New methods of agriculture, especially crop rotation, helped farmers to make their land more productive as they no longer left one-third of their land fallow each year. Selling cash crops was the main source of money for their rent. Potatoes and new agricultural processes brought increased health, nutrition and income, and were seen as a blessing by poor farmers everywhere.

But this blessing became a curse, and Europe and America learned a difficult lesson in the 1840s, when a fungal potato blight, *phytopthera infestans*, first infected the potato crop on the east coast of the United States of America, and as far north as Canada.

Although this blight caused serious hardship, it was not the only staple food for the population, which had access to maize, beans and other grains. However, in Europe the poorest Irish, English and Scottish farmers had come to rely on the potato, and in the 1840s there were only four varieties of potato in common use. This phenomenon was very close to what we now call 'mono-cropping', a dangerous situation where one crop is grown so extensively that, when anything happens to the harvest, its affects can be devastating.

Potato blight is a fungus and like all fungi needs a very specific level of moisture, temperature and darkness. The persistent summer rain of 1845, together with intermittent sunny spells warming the soil, combined with cool, moist nights, created ideal conditions for the blight to thrive.

No one in Ireland suspected that the unusually warm, wet weather in July and the resulting dark, moist soil were ideal for the growth of this fungus. But by September 1845, the warmer south-eastern counties of Ireland – Waterford and Wexford – discovered that their potatoes were rotting in the ground and their crop had been destroyed.

As word spread, farmers in neighbouring counties quickly dug up their crops to salvage as much of the potato harvest as possible, and around half the country was found to have been infected. Ireland, with its history of warm, damp summer weather, was used to losing part of the crop, but this was the worst failure that had ever been recorded.

Sir Robert Peel, the prime minister of Great Britain, responded to the 1845 potato crop failure in Ireland by quickly purchasing £100,000 worth of maize and cornmeal from the United States of America to send to Ireland. He immediately fell foul of the infamous Corn Laws, the first of which was enacted in 1815, and the government was taxed heavily for importing this grain. So even during the worst of the famine in Ireland, it was still possible to buy food if you had enough money.

The Irish nicknamed the maize 'Peel's Brimstone' because of its bright sulphurous-yellow colour. They knew from the letters they received from their relations in America that maize was mainly grown to feed animals. Although it could be eaten directly from the cob, it was usually ground into flour – a tedious process – before being made into a gruel-like porridge. It was not as nutritious as potatoes, and people who depended on it sometimes developed scurvy.[1]

This maize was imported into Ireland at a time when Ireland was still exporting food to England. Why, when the Irish people were starving, was Ireland still a net exporter of food? This is a simple question – still asked today about world trade – with a complex answer.

In 1845, the extremely unpopular Corn Laws were still

in place. These laws were designed to keep the price of corn artificially high in England, to prevent the importation of cheaper foreign grains, mostly from America, and to soothe the demands of British farmers who were not as well off as their counterparts working in the industrial cities. Import duties were so high, that cheap grains from overseas were just as expensive to buy in England as English corn. Despite these laws, poor grain harvests in England sometimes meant that Irish grain had to be imported at a lower price – this was possible because at the time Ireland was part of the United Kingdom and not subject to their international trade laws.

Peel was also under pressure from Richard Cobden and John Bright of the Anti-Corn Law League, who were arguing for Free Trade and the repeal of the Corn Laws. In the early 1840s, the working classes in England were almost as hungry as the Irish. As one English farm labourer said during the Free Trade campaign: 'I be protected [by the Corn Laws] and I be starving.'[2]

John Bright (1811–1889) was a British Radical and later a Liberal, who was involved in the formation of the Anti-Corn Law League and was a champion of land rights for the Irish throughout his career. Often unpopular with many of his peers for his strong and eloquent condemnation of British foreign policy, he was nonetheless considered one of the greatest orators of his time.

Most surprisingly, the Corn Laws were economic laws, at a time when England followed an ideology of *laissez-faire* – roughly translated as not interfering with the economy, or leaving things be – in terms of economic policy. The *laissez-faire* philosophy stated that not only was it wrong for the government to interfere with economic laws, but it was also futile to do so.[3]

Landlords of Irish country estates in the 1840s were often heavily indebted and held crippling mortgages, often from living beyond their means. There had been a growing 'property bubble' in the previous decade, when rents and land prices had increased significantly in Ireland. Landlords secured their large mortgages on these over-valued lands and the increasing income they received from their tenants. Land in Ireland came at a premium, because unlike in England, Irish tenants were prized for always paying their rents. This was evidenced by the numbers who chose to pay their rents rather than buy food during famine times. However, the development of vast swathes of arable land in America and Russia was flooding the European markets with cheap grain. This forced the price of Irish grain down at a time when landlords were gradually ratcheting up their rents. This meant that landlords were desperate – and therefore harsh – when collecting rents from their tenants. In the nineteenth century, stealing and non-payment of debts were considered to be amongst the worst of crimes and were severely punishable by imprisonment, deportation and execution.

In 1845 the harvests were good in England, but in response to the news of the potato crop failure in Ireland Peel proposed the opening of British ports to foreign corn in an effort to feed the starving Irish. This policy was condemned at a meeting of the Friends of Ireland in Boston in December 1845:

It appears by undoubted evidence, recently arrived among us, that the British Government neglects to provide for the inevitable famine which impends of the Irish people by refusing to shut the Irish ports against the further exportation of the grain grown upon the soil, which belongs by the laws of God to the Irish people, but on the contrary, induces the export of Irish Grain to England by keeping up the inhuman Corn Laws, and forbidding the reception of foreign Wheat, Flour or Corn into the United Kingdom, unless on payment of an agricultural duty.[4]

The Anti-Corn Law League leaped on the Irish famine and the international criticism of the Corn Laws to hold massive demonstrations throughout England, and on 25 June 1846 the Corn Laws were repealed. However, Peel was considered to have committed 'political suicide' by supporting Free Trade, and he was forced to resign five days later.[5] Had he waited a little longer he might have been vindicated, as the anticipated drop in corn prices never happened, and landowners and farmers alike breathed a sigh of relief.

It was the combination of political action by the Anti-Corn Law League, Peel's change of heart and grassroots action by farmers and working class activists, which led to the change in law. The rotting potatoes of the Irish famine were the final factor, although critics suggest that instead of tapering the Corn Laws out over a three-year period, as Peel did, he should have repealed them immediately. Regardless, this decision cost him his job as prime minister.

Irish nationalists followed this issue with interest, and learned how effective the combination of political pressure and action by the masses can be. However, they were exhausted from a three-year battle to survive, and still recovering from the humiliating defeat of the Young Irelander's rebellion in 1848, to do anything about it. But this knowledge was absorbed, to be resurrected when the time was right.

WAR IN THE AMERICAS

While Delia Parnell nursed her growing family of six young children, with another on the way in 1848, she kept a watchful eye on what was happening in the United States, her homeland.

As the potato blight caused trouble and starvation in Ireland, in the United States the Mexican War of 1846–1848 was raging. Slavery was the big issue of the day, with the profitability of the cotton plantations depending on unpaid labour in the form of slavery, in much the same way that the profitability of Irish country estates depended on Irish farm labourers who were in effect labouring just to pay their rents. The major result of the Mexican War was an expanded United States. Established states came into conflict over whether or not these new territories would be constituted as free labour states or slave states. The southern states felt strongly that the territories were amenable to slavery. Pro-slavery politicians and businessmen pushed to include New Mexico, parts of California and Utah as slave states, enlarging the total number of states in the future Confederacy and unsettling the balance between slave and free states.

The Fenian movement, ever watchful of armed insurrection in other countries, watched the Mexican War with interest. They, too, felt that Irish tenants were in a type of servitude that was similar to slavery in Mexico. Britain's now arch-enemy, the United States, was about to grow stronger. Encouraged by this, Young Ireland staged an uprising in Ireland in 1848. It was doomed to failure before it even began, as plans were leaked and became common knowledge. This was a year of an international revolutionary wave, as 1848 also saw uprisings in Italy, France, Prussia, Hungary, Greater Poland and Germany.

Delia, although busy with her growing family, and tired from her continued pregnancies, kept her mind occupied with news from around the world. Encouraged by the example of her own well-travelled mother, Delia was determined to keep abreast of current affairs so that her children would not be constrained by their geographical limits and would learn about the world.

The Parnell family, who had a keen interest in current affairs, would have followed all the key social issues of the day. The industrial revolution had brought with it the new problem of an urban population explosion and unexpected epidemics of cholera and typhoid which affected wealthy and poor alike. In the 1840s, the British government was much more concerned with the public health risk of over-crowded cities than it was with the growing unrest in the countryside. Urban working-class poverty became the focus of the legislature in this newly industrialised country, for many reasons.

The Houses of Parliament were situated in London, one of the worst slum-ridden areas in the country. The smell of open sewers, dirty water, cooking fires, smog and horses filled the air, and city dwellers dreamed of living in the wide, open countryside. Hygiene and food quality were also poor, and over-crowding caused contagious diseases, such as tuberculosis, to infect entire families.

Industrialists made their wealth from the new manufacturing industry, and as a result needed to keep their workers in good health to grow profits. Others, of a more charitable nature, were deeply disturbed by the appalling conditions in which the workers' families lived. Regardless of the motives, the government's focus was on solving the problems of the urban poor. The rural poor were considered fortunate by comparison to their city cousins.

Vast factories and mills were situated in northern England, where the cool, moist climate was best suited to the manufacture of delicate cotton threads. However, conditions for workers in factories were so injurious to health, that the average age of death for a worker in Manchester was just seventeen years. *The Blue Books*[6] of 1844–1845 revealed that although Britain was the world leader in industrial development, living conditions of the working classes were so horrendous that the annual death-rate from typhus fever was 'double that of the fatalities of the allied armies at Waterloo'.[7]

In the 1840s, Britain itself was what is now referred to as a developing country.[8] The population had grown to 18.5 million, which was an increase of three-quarters in forty years.

Malpass and Murie (1987) describe urban growth resulting from penniless farmers abandoning their land for the promise of work in the cities:

> ... smoke and fumes filled the atmosphere, and noxious effluent drained into the rivers ... towns quickly became grossly congested, polluted and unhealthy places to live and work. Thus, ironically, the very centres of wealth production in the world's richest country were themselves squalid and unsanitary.

The cities of England were becoming nothing more than overcrowded slums. As well as poor water and sewerage systems, the poor lived in dwellings described by Malpass and Murie as 'small, damp, badly ventilated, deprived of daylight and sometimes structurally unsound'. Even hovels close to centres of employment attracted a high rent, leading to gross over-crowding as tenants took in lodgers to help pay the rent.

Although poverty was not a major concern in itself to the authorities, they did have a nagging fear of a possible rebellion by these brutalised masses. The real threat was epidemics of diseases caused by poor water supply and sanitation. These diseases travelled by water, even into the homes of the middle classes, and infectious illnesses such as typhus and tuberculosis became epidemics because people were so crowded together.

Sick employees were not productive employees either; penniless widows and orphans were a burden on the over-stretched 'poor relief' facilities, and diseases which affected all social classes required more than a *laissez-faire* approach to solve them. The state had no choice but to intervene.

FAMINE RELIEF EFFORTS

The state also intervened in Ireland during the famine. Employment schemes were set up to encourage people to earn a wage and use this money to buy food. The jobs were often hard, manual labour that burned more calories than the meagre wage could make up for in food. Labourers were paid by the volume of work they did, not the hours, so the weaker a worker became, the less he was paid. Labourers were forced to abandon working their farms to earn money to buy food, and had to delay planting their crops for the next season.

Britain tried other solutions in turn, such as direct aid, private charities, Poor Law taxes, public works and soup kitchens. A network of successful soup kitchens eventually fed three million people, but was closed down after six months because of fears that people would become over-dependent on it.

Eventually, under Sir Charles Trevelyan (the assistant secretary to the treasury in London, and the British civil servant responsible for famine relief) England withdrew direct aid entirely and made the disastrous decision of leaving famine relief to private enterprise. Trevelyan commented in a letter dated 9 October 1846 to the Right Honourable Lord Mounteagle that: 'I must beg of you to dismiss all doubt from your mind of the magnitude of the existing calamity and its danger not being fully known and appreciated in Downing Street.'[9]

Trevelyan then goes on to praise the work of the official famine relief agencies: 'The government establishments are strained to do the utmost to alleviate this great calamity and avert this danger, as far as it is in the power of government to do so.' He then says that he had never before seen 'such hearty and cordial co-operation'.

He explains why, despite the fact that this relief was working so well, he was going to withdraw it and argues that famine relief should not be paid for by the government, but should be undertaken by the landlords who, through their greed, were mostly to blame for the disaster. 'The nobility and gentry have met in their respective baronies,' says Trevelyan, 'and beyond making presentments required by law, they have, with rare exceptions, confined themselves to memorials and deputations calling upon the government to do everything, as if they have themselves no part in this great crisis of the country.'

In common with the Victorian thinking, Trevelyan believed in *laissez-faire* and applied it squarely to Ireland: 'It forms no part of the functions of government to provide supplies of food or to increase the productive powers of the land. In the great institutions of the business of society, if falls to the share of government to protect the merchant and the agriculturist in the free exercises of their respective employments, but not to carry out these employments.'

The quote from Trevelyan's letter, however, which has been most frequently used, is his remark that the famine was 'the direct stroke of an all-wise Providence in a manner as unexpected and unthought as it is likely to be effectual' in encouraging landlords to 'take the lead which their position requires' to prevent a 'social revolution' in Ireland. Trevelyan's comments, which could be interpreted to mean that God sent the famine to Ireland, have reverberated through Irish history.

In the context of the day, however, social revolution, in the manner of the French Revolution, was the most feared of all social unrest in Britain. The threat of a violent uprising of millions of Irish people, hundreds and thousands of whom were already living in rural England and London, was a terrifying prospect.

Although Anna Parnell would not have seen this letter, she was clear about the causes of the famine and what should have been done about it. Anna later wrote in her *Tale*:

> There was enough food to maintain the large population of 1847 … and even where there was least there were still only a few who had too little. But the failure of one crop, the potato, in 1846, was enough to sweep away all that tenants had left to maintain themselves on after paying their rents.

She continued:

> In 1846, the tenants sold all they had to pay the landlords and then lay down to die, making their wives and children do the same. The question naturally arises, why, with the food actually in their own hands, the cultivators of the soil did not feed themselves first? It seems a hard question to answer, and

yet there is more than one answer to it. If they had not paid their rent, they would have been evicted, and then would have perished of cold, exposure and starvation combined … the workhouses in Ireland could only meet the demands made on them in 'prosperous times' … it does not seem possible that even the English government could prevent … millions of people from holding onto … the food, fuel and miserable hovels there were in possession of.

The true depth of Anna's feelings about the famine, and her view on the British response, reveals much about her character, and the motivation for her future work with the Ladies' Land League:

But if the Irish choose to do anything of which the English disapprove, such as eating, for instance, when they are intended to starve, they must face the prospect of wholesale massacre, and though it may seem that a chance of massacre ought to be better than the certainty of starvation, those who have not had to face both alternatives are not in the best position to judge their respective charms.

Anna's ideas about what happened to all the funds that were raised around the world for the starving Irish are equally stark:

It is possible, also, that the Irish looked to charity to pull them through. If so, their judgement, to a certain extent, was correct, for the peoples of the world subscribed more than enough to cope with the famine. But with some trivial exceptions, this provision proved useless, as most of the money found its way into the hands of the English government, and never found it out again.

But Irish peasants, trusting to the very end, sold the grains they had grown and faithfully paid what rent they could, and trusted in God, their landlords, the British government, the Poor Laws and their fellow Irish neighbours to fill their bellies. But their trust was misplaced and by 1851, the year before Anna Parnell was born, there were two million fewer people in Ireland, and the population had dropped from eight million in the census of 1841, to six million in the census of 1851. Despite the efforts of an army of volunteers, the usual safety nets which had worked so well in the past buckled one by one under the demands placed on them. Eviction, starvation, disease and emigration decimated the population.

In 1852, Anna Parnell was still a baby, and her older brother, the future Irish statesman, Charles Stewart Parnell, who celebrated his sixth birthday on 27 June, was playing with his toys in the nursery. Both children were safely protected from the injustices of the world around them. As soon as they were old enough to understand, they would learn all about it from their mother Delia, who was an active and socially conscious young woman. Although Delia's time was mostly taken up with running the home and caring for her children, she astutely observed what was going on in the Irish countryside. The dislike of the English, which Delia had learned at her own father's knee, grew even deeper.

She often spoke at length to her children about the world outside Ireland, and reminisced about her colourful childhood and her parent's adventures, such as the time Anna and Charles' Grandma Delia visited the court of Napoleon and Josephine in Paris in the early 1800s, or the horror of 1812, when Grandma Delia faced internment in London as an American citizen when war broke out between England and America.

Given their family history of involvement in international conflict between America and England, it is hardly surprising that the young Parnells – particularly Charles, Anna and Fanny – took an active interest in politics throughout their lives.

In their nursery, or cuddled up with their mother in front of the fire after supper, the children listened to stories of their brave grandfather, the American naval hero Commodore Charles Stewart, and their vivacious society belle grandmother, Mrs Delia Stewart.

Born in Philadelphia on 17 July 1778, the young Charles Stewart headed off to sea at the age of thirteen for a life of adventure as a cabin boy in the merchant navy. A bright young boy with a mind for business, he worked his way up through the ranks, making a substantial fortune in his early thirties working as a merchant seaman from 1808 to 1812, until war broke out with England. He eventually joined the United States Navy. In November 1813, he married Miss Delia Tudor and shortly afterwards, at the age of thirty-five, he returned to sea as captain of the frigate USS *Constitution*.

It is just as well he spent a lot of time at sea, because various historical sources agree that the two were never compatible, and it is probably the enforced absences which enabled their marriage to last for ten years.

In February 1815, as he was sailing off the coast of Portugal, he encountered two English ships, the *Levant* and the *Cyane*, and after a daring sea battle, he captured both. None of the three ships involved in this skirmish were aware that the war had officially ended a few months earlier, but since communication with ships at sea had always been slow, this was not unusual for the time. In a gentlemanly fashion, the three captains discussed the finer points of their battle over a drink in the triumphant Captain Charles Stewart's cabin.

This heroic exploit made him a celebrity back in America, but the press soon turned its attention to the news in Europe. The Emperor Napoleon Bonaparte had returned from the island of Elba after his eleven-year exile, and marched on Paris. The English and Prussian allies declared war on France again, and the Duke of Wellington from Britain and General Blucher from Prussia engaged Napoleon at the Battle of Waterloo. Napoleon's final bid for power ended with defeat and the newspapers reported the great loss of life on both sides.

Later that year, the dashing captain bought a 225 acre estate, which became known as 'Old Ironsides', the affectionate nickname that had been given to his ship and which later became a nickname for the man himself. He went back to sea again for two years. While he was away, in 1817, he was promoted to the rank of commodore.

When he returned to Ironsides, he discovered that his wife Delia had sold much of the household contents to pay for her lifestyle expenses. Furious, he brought his wife and children on his next posting to the Pacific, where they lived in Lima, a coastal town in Peru, South America.

Delia enjoyed her time there, and her gift for languages enabled her to act as her husband's interpreter, and to translate his letters into French and Spanish. She was an outgoing young wife, who revelled in the endless round of diplomatic parties.

Delia was also very naïve, and was persuaded by some friends to smuggle a man on board her husband's ship the USS *Franklin*. Unknown to her, or her friends, the man was a Spanish spy, and the incident was nearly the ruination of her husband. America had been carefully trying to stay neutral in the war between Spain and the Spanish colonies in South America, and assisting a spy to escape was enough to cause international outrage.

The commodore was hauled before a court-martial and threatened with being stripped of his rank. He pleaded with Delia to admit what had happened. It was difficult for her to explain that she had – unwittingly or otherwise – smuggled a Spanish spy on board her husband's ship. The commodore was sent to Washington to explain his actions, while the Peruvian authorities demanded to know what was going on. The court-martial hung over the commodore's head for almost a year before Delia was finally persuaded to testify, and their relationship suffered as a result.

When she returned some months later to the family estate,

she discovered that she had been thrown out of the house by her husband. She was forced to battle for many years for custody of the children and financial support for herself.

In 1828, Delia Stewart and her twelve-year-old daughter, also named Delia, visited Washington and were invited to tea with President John Quincy Adams. Delia was delighted at the attention that both she and her daughter received. A proud mother, she commented at the time that 'little Delia, as if made for such circles, was the charm of all'. Thus began young Delia's love of being the centre of attention at parties.

Young Delia had her first offer of marriage when she was sixteen, but declined. By the time she was seventeen, another proposal was made, this time by John Parnell, an Anglo-Irish gentleman, who was twenty-two years of age, and touring America with his cousin, Lord Powerscourt. John Parnell was scrutinised by the entire Stewart family, and his quiet demeanour, sober tastes and love of the countryside were found to be acceptable. Miss Delia Stewart became Mrs Delia Parnell on 31 May 1835, when she was nineteen. Ten days later, the newlyweds set off for London.

Despite the possible scandals of the court-martial and the commodore's long term affair with a 'pretty young married countrywoman' – which was mentioned in a letter from Anna's grandmother Delia to her great-uncle William in 1826 – he was later awarded a gold medal for gallantry, good conduct, and services by the Congress of the United States. He was so popular that in 1838 his name was put forward as a Democratic candidate for the American presidency. It is interesting to note that their famous grandfather had not been negatively affected by his affair with a married woman, whereas during the reign of Queen Victoria, morality came under very close scrutiny and led to the ultimate downfall of some political leaders.

These were the family histories that Anna and all the Parnell children heard at their proud mother's knee. Stories of adventure on the high seas, fortunes to be won, life in the court of the Emperor Napoleon in France and afternoon tea with the president of the United States. The simple life in the beautiful estate of Avondale just couldn't compare with the glamour of the life their mother had lost, at least not in her own eyes. Delia Parnell spent many years yearning to revisit the excitement of her youth. Little did she realise that her own children would be the catalysts that would bring her once again to prominence in her beloved home country.

Despite the horrors of the recently ended famine, 1852, the year Anna Parnell was born, was a good time to look back over the achievements of the previous half-century. Many things were cheaper and better than before: the Penny Post had revolutionised communication, there were more building materials, more fabrics, more pottery and cooking utensils available.

The main streets in most of the larger towns were now paved and gas-lighting was being introduced, making travel at night safer. Trains, trams, carriages and bridges made travel much easier, and faster. Living standards rose as food, clothing, medicines and furniture became more affordable.

It wasn't just agriculture that was changing – economic theories which had once seemed so solid, now failed as the industrial revolution re-wrote the rule book. Mechanical devices, giant looms, massive printing presses, manufacturing processes and improved distribution meant that goods could be produced faster, cheaper and to a more consistent quality than ever before. Goods which previously were confined to local markets could now reach regional markets, regional markets became national markets, and national markets became international markets. It seemed to industrialists that the world was indeed their oyster. As fast as goods could be produced, they were consumed. The falling costs of production meant that more goods were becoming accessible to the poor.

A spirit of humanitarianism had overcome the *laissez-faire* attitude, and new legislation to protect public health, factory workers and miners was enacted. There was much to hope for.

But beneath this 'façade of peace and plenty there still existed squalor and ignorance, poverty and degradation, sweat-shops and slums' in the cities.[10] And in the countryside, although the plight of agricultural workers improved a little, they still appeared to be 'swept like a heap of rubbish into a corner'.[11]

Although all seemed peaceful, the Irish spirit had been only temporarily broken by the Great Famine. Anna Parnell later wrote:

> Even to persons who were not in existence when they occurred, the horrors of these years [the Irish Potato Famine] had a vividness almost as great as actual experience of them could

produce … in spite of money and food both in plenty, the famine and the diseases bred of it ran riot – unchecked for years.

Nationalists had learned a great deal from the successes and failures of other mass movements for freedom and equality across Europe. It was not long before the battle for Irish independence began once again.

2

A Cosmopolitan Childhood

The Victorian era was a time of rapid transformation in Ireland, Britain and across Europe. Expanding rail networks and steamships made international travel easier, and transatlantic travel was no longer a life-threatening journey.

Globalisation as we know it had begun. Goods could travel from all corners of the earth, and vast fortunes could be made in shipping and distribution. Transport was now so rapid that exotic fruits and vegetables and livestock could be easily brought to the tables of those who could afford expensive delicacies.

Ideas, too, began to travel more widely, as people, books and periodicals crossed the oceans. Compulsory education led to a growing literate population hungry for new material to read; the steam engine made possible the mechanised mass production of cheap books and periodicals, and electricity brought the ability to work and read late into the night. Europe and America devoured exciting new ideas in science fiction, evolution, human behaviour and the limitless possibilities of a good life for all.

But, at the same time, the vast majority of the population was trapped in meaningless work in filthy factories or struggling for survival tilling the land. The good life was only in the reach of the wealthy and the powerful elite. It was only a matter of time before the population realised that this was unfair and unjust.

And so, the seeds of civil unrest were planted across Europe. Peasants and artisans were unhappy with the ceaseless influx of cheap food and goods from other countries, which ate into their own markets. Little by little, the working families of Europe became poorer and poorer, even though they were working harder and harder, and inequality between rich and poor became even more blatant.

Populations across Western Europe were becoming restless, and the rumblings of republican and socialist dissent began. Peasants were no longer happy handing over their hard-earned cash to their landlords: they wanted the chance to own their own land, to reap the rewards for their work, and to enjoy the good life that seemed so unjustly out of their reach.

Civil activists learned from America that it was possible to gain a better life for yourself and your family through the rewards of your own work. What was it the Americans were doing that wasn't being done in Europe? The discussion polarised in two opposite ends of the 'development' spectrum. At one end were the concepts of socialism and communism for collective betterment, and at the other end the American Dream of using the market to allow individuals to lift themselves from poverty.

In Ireland a combination of both these philosophies flourished: the idea of the collective tenants of Ireland claiming the right of ownership over their own land, and then using market strategies so that each family could seek to improve their standard of living.

REBUILDING A NEW IRELAND AFTER THE FAMINE

When Queen Victoria visited Ireland in 1853 at the age of thirty-four, four years after her first visit, the famine was long over, and there were visible signs of improvement as life slowly returned to normal. Her visit was well received, and fears of a civil uprising were put aside. The young Queen's popularity was as high as ever, and there were reports that even some nationalists at party meetings ended by singing *God Save the Queen*.

However, affection for the Queen was not enough to completely quell civil unrest; it was still alive in the hearts of the Irish who had escaped on the infamous famine ships to America and Europe and it resurfaced again in the future. But for now, years of famine, disease and harsh winters had temporarily broken the Irish spirit, and the struggle for survival took precedence over national independence. In the 1850s, 'the mass of the people, preoccupied with the struggle for survival, had neither the energy nor the spirit to struggle for national independence.'[1]

THE COSMOPOLITAN PARNELL FAMILY

It was in this new Ireland that the Parnell family, with its unique understanding and knowledge of the Irish, American and British psyches, positioned itself. Born of an American mother and Anglo-Irish father, Anna was a true cosmopolitan – a citizen of the world – although she would always consider herself to be Irish.

Despite the tragedy of her brother Hayes' death in 1854, Anna's early childhood was happy, filled with sporty, outdoor activities and fresh air with her brothers and sisters, mainly at Avondale, and mostly in the 'comforting presence' of her father John and their nannies according to historian Jane McL. Côté.[2] She describes their 'easy-going and affectionate' mother, Delia, who was busy with the older children, particularly the girls. Anna's parents, although they never divorced, had become estranged after the death of their eldest son. As John and Delia spent more and more time apart, Delia had focused her energies on attending to the education of her surviving children, particularly her daughters. John had strong views on the importance of a good education, and Delia was fortunate to be able to send her daughters to finishing schools in London and Paris. This was also an excellent pretext for Delia to visit these cities and participate in the social seasons, much to her delight.

Although theories of education were changing, it was still often seen as the father's role to educate only his sons. As Côté so eloquently puts it, 'as an upper class Victorian matron it was very much [Delia's] right and duty to establish her daughters in society, first by ensuring that they acquired the stock of social graces necessary to ornament a drawing-room and then by bringing them out during the Season where they would with good luck and good management find a suitable husband.'

John, in contrast to Delia, preferred a life outdoors, and enjoyed cricket and riding in particular, so was happy to remain home in his beloved Avondale, as the 'warm and distant sun around which the life of the estate revolved'. He was also drawn into local affairs, and his time serving as a Poor Law Guardian would have made him deeply aware of the divide between wealth and poverty in the county of Wicklow.

Food at Avondale was plentiful and nourishing, but basic. Clothing was warm, practical and modest. John, a member of the Church of Ireland, instilled in his young family a strong sense of right and wrong, and he was very strict in his observance of Sunday as the Sabbath day. The children studied the Bible, and in their future writings and speeches, were able to quote liberally from scripture. Delia, who loved the social whirl of dressing up for balls and banquets, found John's austerity a little difficult, which probably also explains the brevity of her infrequent visits to Avondale.

Behind the scenes, their father John made some efforts to ensure the financial future of his large family. His second son, Charles, he decided, would inherit Avondale. His eldest son, John, would inherit an estate called Collure, from which the girls' meagre annuities would be paid. And finally, he borrowed an enormous sum of money to purchase an estate for his youngest son, Henry.

But Anna's blissful early childhood, running free through the forests and glades of Avondale under the genial eye of her father, and punctuated with exciting adventures to the wondrous cities of London and Paris with her mother, was soon shattered by tragedy.

When she was barely seven years old, Anna's father died suddenly on 3 July 1858. He was forty-eight. He had been playing cricket in Dublin when he became ill and died in hospital. At the time Anna, her mother and all of her siblings except Charles were in Paris. Their father's death certificate simply stated that he died of 'inflammation of the bowel'.

Young Charles, then only thirteen years old, attended his father's funeral alone. Their father had only recently amended his will. Unfortunately, this was not to secure his family's future in the event of his death, but to cut his young daughter Emily out of it. John had heard from his sister in London, Lady Howard, that Emily was attracting the wrong kind of suitor during her season – a Mr Arthur Monroe Dickinson in particular.

Côté notes that: 'Like other energetic and headstrong men, John Parnell had made his will without any thought of actually dying until such a time as he should find it convenient to do so.' The will created, 'lasting bitterness in his wife and those of his children who believed, with reason, that they had been unfairly treated.'

In the Parnell family, as was common in many landowning families, only the men were wealthy; their wives and sisters were totally financially dependent on their husbands and brothers. To each of his daughters and his wife John left an annuity of £100, a small amount even then, although there was a clause providing for the girls' continuing education. He forgot to make his wife Delia the guardian of their children, and he also made no provision to pay maintenance for his family in the event of his death before his second son Charles was old enough to inherit the family estate of Avondale. John Howard Parnell, the eldest son in the family, was the logical heir to the estate at Avondale, but as Côté remarked:

> He stammered as a child and lacked the imperious and lively character of his younger brother Charles, a more suitable heir in his father's eyes, to the proud though recent tradition of the Parnells of Avondale.

Young John was therefore bequeathed the 'unproductive estate of Collure' instead of Avondale, and it was from Collure that all the Parnell women's income was supposed to be paid.

Delia also discovered that a huge debt of £65,000 had been added to the Parnell books to pay for the estate for their youngest son Henry. The accounts were in a state of total confusion so it was hardly surprising to discover after John's death that the Parnell finances were in a perilous state.

This meant that Delia suddenly found herself not only widowed, but virtually destitute and with no way to support a large family for at least the next four years until her eldest son John inherited his meagre estate, and possibly for the next eight years, until Charles was twenty-one and inherited Avondale.

Moreover, to keep custody of her children, Delia had to make them Wards of Court. She was not impressed, but also not particularly surprised, about this disastrous lack of planning by her husband.[3]

To balance the books, the Parnell family were forced to move out of Avondale. The estate was rented to tenants while they in turn lived in a rented house in Dalkey. This was not entirely unpleasant, however, as Dalkey was a beautiful Georgian coastal town, just south of Dublin, the capital city. The family enjoyed living by the sea and swimming off the rocks. They were also on good terms with the tenant at Avondale and had a small house on the estate where they could stay and enjoy familiar surroundings. Less than a year later, the family moved closer to Dublin, to another rented house on the coast, this time in Kingstown (Dun Laoghaire).

Anna grew up dependent on her mother's support and the provisions of her father's unsatisfactory will; the relative wealth of the men in her family compared to the financial struggles of the women informing her view of how the uneven distribution of wealth was a major contributor to social injustice. The Parnell family's wealth lay mainly in the estate at Avondale and the land was inherited by her sons with only a small annuity secured on the land to her daughters. Delia therefore knew from early on that her daughters would not be able to bring a dowry to their marriages and would need to find a husband solely on their own merits as charming, educated young ladies. This is one of the reasons why Delia focused so much attention on the girls' education and social skills; it was, quite literally, all they would have.

Delia was determined that her daughters would make good marriages, despite the odds stacked against them, but that would ultimately prove to be a futile hope. Lady Howard, Delia's great-aunt, took one of Delia's daughters, also called Delia, under her wing for her first Season in London in 1855, and was delighted to report that the young woman would be presented to Queen Victoria the following spring with the other debutantes. But even after this promising start, her lack of a fortune resulted in young Delia marrying a man she did not love.

Anna Parnell's American roots, and her mother's politics, shaped her young mind into accepting the deep contradictions of her heritage. Michael Kimmel describes how American women like Delia had greater freedom than women in Europe in the nineteenth century, by observing that 'without dowries to tie them economically to their families, and with the right to own property in their own names after marriage, American women had an easier time both marrying and re-marrying.'[4] In the pioneering nineteenth century, American and other colonial families were radically different to those in the more traditional Anglo-Irish society.[5] In America, marriages were increasingly based on love-matches, where Kimmel reports a 'surge of sentiment' which encouraged men and women to marry on the basis of mutual affection, rather than the colder sentiment of a 'union of two lineages'.

But family life in America was changing by the mid 1800s. Women and men, who until then mostly worked together in and around their homes, were also being affected by the move from what Kimmel describes as the 'rhythm of family time' and into 'industrial time'.

By the 1850s, even literature was polarising into men's (industrial, scientific) and women's (home-based, romantic) interest. This sentiment was echoed in the novels of authors such as Jane Austen (1775–1817) who remained popular throughout the entire nineteenth century. George Eliot (Mary Ann [Marian] Evans), herself a popular novelist, wrote a scathing attack on the popular literature of the time in an essay called *Silly Novels by Lady Novelists*, describing the 'mind-and-millinery' species of novel, with a heroine who 'is usually an heiress, probably a peeress in her own right, with perhaps a vicarious baronet, an amiable duke and an irresistible younger son of a marquis in the foreground, a clergyman and a poet sighing for her in the middle distance, and a crowd of undefined adorers simply indicated beyond'. The first type of heroine most despised by Eliot was the heiress whose 'eyes and her wit are both dazzling; her nose and her morals are alike free from any tendency to irregularity; she has a superb contralto and a superb intellect; she is perfectly well-dressed and perfectly religious; she dances like a sylph, and reads the Bible in the original tongues'. The other clichéd heroine 'is not an heiress … but she infallibly gets into high society, she has the triumph of refusing many matches and securing the best, and she wears some family jewels or other as a sort of crown of righteousness at the end'.

Anna Parnell is always described as a very well-read young lady, who would no doubt have discovered works by Jane Austen and George Eliot on her mother's bookshelves, or perhaps hidden them in her desk or under her pillow like a lot of young ladies to avoid derision. Certainly, the library at Avondale was a 'great treasure house of knowledge' according to Côté, in which Anna acquired 'a vast knowledge of Irish and

English history, political economy, church history and English, French and American literature'. But very little is known about her own personal life. There was one whisper of a possible suitor in Rathdrum reported by Côté, but apart from that, nothing. Anna, with her negative impression of marriage from her mother, seemed to have focused her attentions on her studies, her painting and her political work. There was little time for romance in her life.

As life and literature mirrored each other, men continued to leave the home to work in industrialised surroundings like factories, shops, offices and mills. Women, still bound by their biology to childbirth and child-rearing, remained in the home, and their work was, according to Kimmel, 'as exalted in popular literature as it was potentially imprisoning in reality'. Women became trapped in the home by the new ideology of feminine domesticity, at the same time as men became excluded and exiled from it. Kimmel describes how women's work was 'reconceptualised, not as work at all, but rather as a God-given mission'. Child-rearing, traditionally undertaken by whichever parent was the same sex as the child, was now seen as entirely women's work.

French writer Alexis de Tocqueville described the American family home as the 'haven in a heartless world'. The nineteenth-century home became a 'site of sentimentalised longing' where feminine domesticity was kept in place by 'ideological buttressing from rhapsodic poetry and religious sermons'. But these revolutionary new ideas about gender roles, which had their roots in America, and which Delia Parnell brought with her to Ireland, fitted the emerging social structures in industrialised Europe very well.

Of course, this didn't apply to every family – it was a white, middle-class phenomenon. Working-class women in America, as throughout Europe, continued to work both inside and outside the home, out of economic necessity. The romanticised ideal was not within everyone's reach.

CIVIL WAR IN AMERICA

In 1860, Grandma Delia visited from America to provide support to her widowed daughter and eight grandchildren. She was also deeply worried about the possibility of a civil war in America. There was political deadlock between the predominantly agricultural, slave-holding states in the south and the industrialised, free labour states in the north.

President Buchanan was trying to preserve the Union, which meant being careful not to upset the states in the south, but his efforts at conciliation were perceived as a sign of weakness.

During the election campaign in 1860, Abraham Lincoln campaigned against the expansion of slavery beyond the states in which it already existed. Following the election, and even before Lincoln took office on 4 March 1861, seven southern states declared their secession from the Union. Both the outgoing and incoming US administrations considered secession to be an act of rebellion. The situation quickly deteriorated, and American Civil War finally broke out on 12 April 1861 when Confederate forces attacked the US outpost of Fort Sumter in South Carolina.

Rear Admiral Charles Stewart, now an elderly gentleman of eighty-three, was furious that the Confederates had dared to fire on the flag of the Republic and petitioned to go back on active duty with the navy. The navy declined, so he turned his hand to writing propaganda pamphlets instead.

Anna was only nine when the Civil War broke out, and her sister Fanny was thirteen. The two girls listened with interest to their mother and grandmother's passionate discussions about the situation in America. It was probably at this stage that Anna first drew parallels between the plight of slaves in America and the landless peasantry in Ireland, who were in effect slaving on someone else's land simply to stay alive and pay their rent. Rear Admiral Stewart, Anna's grandfather, owned a large estate in New Jersey. There must have been many long debates within the Parnell household. It is not surprising that Anna and her elder sister Fanny supported the abolition of slavery and the Parnell family strongly supported the Union. This was completely at odds with the English support for the Confederacy. As Côté notes:

> The gentlemanly way of life of the land-owning 'aristocracy' of the South ruling over a servile population was more to their liking than the democratic North where vulgar money-grabbing Yankees presumed to elected office. The *Times* newspaper in London was 'consistently hostile' to the North.

The year 1861 was a difficult one for Queen Victoria, and for the British economy. The American Civil War caused huge disruption to shipping, particularly the export of raw cotton from America. This cotton was essential for the functioning of many of the mills in the north of England. From being the wealthiest country in the world in 1860, the plummeting value of England's cotton trade had the potential to undermine many of the economic gains of the previous decades.

To make matters worse, there was a diplomatic row between Britain and the United States in November 1861, and it was probably only Prince Albert's influence that prevented all-out warfare.[6] That winter, Albert contracted typhoid, a disease of the over-crowded working classes, and died suddenly. Typhoid can only be transmitted from human to human, through contaminated food or water, or poor personal hygiene, and the suggestion was made that it was the Queen's own water supply that had killed Albert.

Although the first Public Health Act of 1848 had been passed to prevent this sort of human tragedy, and the Queen herself had signed various public health acts, at the end of the day it had been the *laissez-faire* approach to health within the royal household that had led to the death of her beloved Albert. Queen Victoria never fully recovered from this devastating personal loss.

EDUCATING THE PARNELL CHILDREN

In 1862, Delia sent Anna's older brothers Charles and John to school in England, to prepare Charles for his entrance exam to Cambridge. Charles succeeded in gaining entry to Cambridge, but left before completing his degree. Delia was still focused on the more practical matter of what to do with her daughters, who were rapidly coming of age. She knew from bitter experience that expensive finishing schools for girls did not guarantee a suitable husband, nor did the pedigree of having an American naval hero for a grandfather. She hired a series of governesses to ensure that Fanny, Anna and Theodosia had at least a minimum education. Undoubtedly it crossed Delia's mind that one or more of her daughters might end up as governesses – one of the few respectable professions for a lady – and being educated by governesses would certainly have been a backup form of training or apprenticeship. Delia knew her daughters would have to depend on their wits, and themselves. A mere £100 a year was not enough to live on.

Fanny, now a young teenager, and bored by her governesses who provided only a minimum education, discovered that she had the ability to write poetry. This, for a time, eased her boredom. She combined her new art form with her political ideas about Irish independence, and this theme began to emerge in her poetry. Anna, encouraged by Fanny, also wrote poetry, but as Côté pointed out, Anna's skill with the pen was more suited to crisp prose than to flowery verse.

In the autumn of 1864, Delia stumbled upon a governess who was able to provide the girls with exactly the kind of serious education that they needed, and they thrived on her stimulating lessons. Indeed, Côté posits that the formal education the girls received from their various governesses, and the informal education they received from their love of books, in many ways exceeded that of their elder brother Charles' college education.

In 1864, Anna's older sister Fanny, then a young woman of only fifteen, began sending some of her poetry to the *Irish People*, a Fenian newspaper. She earned small sums of money writing defiant poems calling for Irish independence, under the pen name of Aleria. She found an eager audience in the rebellious Irish spirit which had travelled with the hundreds and thousands of Irish emigrants and landed on the shores of America.

Although the famine was long over, the tradition of emigration had continued. Remittances from America remained invaluable to the families who had remained in Ireland after the famine. For those who were literate, letters from America contained not only news about the emigrant's health and family, but also stories of easy work and numerous jobs, with the evidence of an exciting new life in the form of hard currency. This money was essential for supporting their families in Ireland. Who could blame the youngest and strongest people of Ireland if, as soon as they were old enough, they too felt the lure of the American gold rush. The British government even went so far as to create schemes to encourage Irish peasants to emigrate.

Irish immigrants found themselves in a world completely different to that which they had left. Federal land laws meant that land could be bought cheaply and easily; at last, Irish men could buy land of their own. And their wives could inherit.

In Ireland, however, despite the welcome influx of regular money from abroad, there was growing unease about the steady haemorrhaging of young, healthy workers to America. This loss of strong labour served to weaken the remaining peasantry, not only in its ability to farm the land productively, but also reduced the number of potential recruits if an armed rebellion was ever to take place. The weak, the sick, the elderly and the very young could not form an army. Perhaps this was the hidden agenda behind the government schemes; no doubt it was debated heavily at Irish Republican Brotherhood (IRB) meetings and within the Parnell household.

The Irish Republican Brotherhood should not have worried that the wholesale emigration of young, healthy Irish people would weaken the Irish spirit. On the contrary, the Irish spirit stayed alive in America, and parents passed on to their children the stories of the unjust life they had led in Ireland. The spirit of rebellion was being passed down to future generations.

The American Civil War, while dividing Anglo-Irish opinion, proved to be an ideal training ground for exiled Irishmen and their descendents. The Irish joined up on both sides in the Civil War, learning the skills and craft of warfare.

That Irishmen fought on both sides of the American Civil War was a cause of great discussion in the Parnell household. The Parnell's felt very differently from the majority of the Irish gentry who broadly supported the Confederate side. Instead, with their unique perspective on the parallels between the enslaved people of African descent and landless Irish peasants, they debated whether warfare could be a solution to the 'Irish Question' as well.

In the summer of 1865, American officers of Irish extraction began to be seen on the streets of Dublin. At first, these returning soldiers were seen as a curiosity, and were ignored by the authorities. However, before long they were recruiting young Irishmen and practising military drills at night. This show of Fenian defiance proved too much for the authorities, and the *Irish People* newspaper offices were raided. Around the country, members of the Irish Republican Brotherhood were arrested and put into prison.

An insurrection of unarmed peasants was one thing, a well-trained army of disgruntled soldiers was something entirely different.

3

London and Parisian Society

Two children playing by a stream,
Two lovers walking in a dream,
A married pair whose dream is o'er,
Two old folks who are quite a bore
'Love's Four Ages' by Anna Parnell (1905)

Even as she attempted to find a solution to the immediate problem of day-to-day living expenses, Delia Parnell knew that the lack of income condemned most of her daughters to a penniless spinsterhood. Without a dowry, it was unlikely that any of them would make good marriages. Dowries had always been a problem in the Parnell family.

Things had gone badly for Anna's eldest sister Delia, now twenty-two, who had married James Livingston Thompson. Delia had spent four seasons attending all the best balls and parties in London and Paris, and had still not been able to find a husband. A beautiful, vibrant young woman, it was probably only her lack of a dowry that prevented her from marrying earlier. Her only hope was to find a wealthy man who would marry her for herself, knowing there would be no marriage portion.

Knowing that there would probably never be another offer as good as this one, in 1859 Delia reluctantly agreed to marry Thompson, a wealthy businessman from a large expatriate community of Americans living in Paris known as the 'American colony'. The colony, in common with their French hosts, shared a distrust of the English, a love of good food and culture, and enjoyed the educational and artistic opportunities to be found in nineteenth-century Paris. By the closing decades of the century, there were as many as 100,000 Americans living in Paris during the high season. In the frank manner of the Parnell women, young Delia made the mistake of admitting to her new husband that she had married him for convenience, and not for love.

Knowing that she did not love him, he quickly became jealous of his pretty young wife, and restricted her freedoms so that she did not even have a horse to enable her to go visiting. Delia, who was not only trapped in a loveless marriage but physically trapped in her own home, decided to end her own life. She chose poison as the method. However, having swallowed the poison, Delia immediately regretted her decision and ran to her young sister Anna, who was visiting her mother in Paris and happened to be there, to beg her for help. Anna was able to save Delia's life by rushing to get assistance, but learned from that moment the consequences of marrying a man one did not love. The impact of witnessing her sister's suicide attempt lingered in the back of her mind. Whatever negative views she may have had about marriage became firmly cemented in her psyche, and she came to view marriage as the end of a dream, and not as a beginning of a life together. In the future, when Anna's personal circumstances became similarly unbearable but for different reasons, suicide presented itself as an option.

Anna's mother knew that she would have to plan carefully to secure husbands for her other five daughters.

PARIS

In the mid-1860s, the youngest of the Parnell children, Fanny, Henry, Anna and Theodosia, spent increasing amounts of time in Paris. Charles, meanwhile, was shipped off yet again to boarding school. For a young man with so many siblings, Charles spent a lot of time on his own. Delia Parnell, tired of struggling to make ends meet in Ireland with four young children, was invited by her brother, Charles Tudor Stewart, to stay with him in Paris for as long as she wished. In common with many European heads of state, Napoleon III was overseeing a programme of urban regeneration, which was, by now, almost completed, and Paris was a magnificent city to behold.

Slum-clearance work in Paris had removed the unsightly – and unsafe – buildings from the vicinity of landmarks such as the Louvre and cathedral of Notre-Dame, and new water supplies had been piped to public fountains for its citizens. As was the fashion, small squares and parks were built as garden oases in the urban filth, giving the illusion, if not the reality, of fresh country air. In the European race to create healthy garden cities and leafy suburbs, this new Paris was, with her wide boulevards and urban planting, quite literally streets ahead.

An American 'colony', which included Charles Tudor Stewart, made its home in this pretty city. Charles Tudor lived on the first floor of 122 Champs-Elysée, a very desirable address. When her son Charles inherited Avondale in 1867 Delia chose to remain in Paris.

Life in Paris was good for the young Parnell family. They lived in one of the most fashionable districts, surrounded by wealthy neighbours – with sons of marriageable age no doubt – and Delia felt completely at home. Côté wrote that the Parnell family was able to indulge in an 'endless round of balls, costume parties, dinners and receptions'. And although their mother clearly enjoyed this, it is not clear whether the young Anna, who had absorbed her father's love of simplicity and virtue and saw herself as Irish rather than American, would really have enjoyed quite so much of what she considered frivolous activity.[1]

Fortunately, Anna was fluent in French and an aspiring artist, and was able to enjoy exhibits in Paris' numerous art galleries and to take lessons. Unfortunately, young ladies were much more closely supervised in Paris than they were in Ireland. The freedoms Anna had enjoyed during her intermittent childhood and adolescent residencies in Avondale, were strictly curtailed in Paris. French culture dictated that a lady's chances of marriage depended very much on her total innocence, and so respectable young women were usually accompanied and chaperoned at all times by a lady's maid.

Anna resented this restriction so much that, despite the wonderful artistic opportunities available for women in Paris, she returned to Dublin when she was eighteen. Four years later, she moved to London to continue her studies in South Kensington. Her father's will made provision for her education, which no doubt he presumed would have ended by the age of twenty, when most ladies of her class were already married. Anna took full advantage of this financial loophole for as long as she could.

In November 1869, Rear Admiral Charles Stewart died at the grand old age of ninety-one. He left the family estate of Ironsides in Bordentown, New Jersey, to his daughter Delia and her brother Charles. The death of her colourful American grandfather and the rumblings of war in Europe made for a difficult winter.

FRANCE DECLARES WAR ON PRUSSIA

The whirling social life of the Parnells and upper-class Paris was cut short in 1870 when diplomatic relationships finally broke down between France and her neighbour Prussia, and eventually Napoleon III declared war.

The American colony was already one step ahead. The day before Napoleon declared war, they had met to decide what the neutral Americans could do in the event that war broke out and – heaven forbid – reached Paris.

It was decided by a committee of twenty-five expatriate Americans to establish a field hospital, which would be known as an American Ambulance, based on the model that had been set up during the American Civil War.

Anna was safely in Ireland, but her sister Fanny and mother Delia were still in Paris. Fanny and Delia were two of the first volunteers for the American Ambulance, and were mentioned by Dr Thomas Evans, the founder of the Ambulance and a famous dentist by trade who had perfected the technique of gold fillings for teeth.[2]

But, like Ireland, France was a Catholic country, which viewed with suspicion any women working outside the home. As Côté reported, nursing was considered, 'despite the activities of Florence Nightingale, as suitable for (presumably) sexless nuns and retired whores'. She further commented that 'the women who came forward were treated to the most extraordinary suspicion and verbal abuse'.

Fanny and Delia spent two months volunteering for the American Ambulance, but were forced to flee Paris on foot with young Theodosia in mid-September, just before the Siege of Paris began.

The siege lasted four months, during which there was a short-lived, but devastating, civil uprising by the socialist Communards, which led to horrendous battles between them and the new government's National Defence army in Paris. The National Defence army hunted down any surviving Communards, and systematically killed, imprisoned or sent them to New Caledonia.

Popular uprisings, like that of the Communards of France, or the one that had long been suggested by the Fenians in Ireland, were risky endeavours. Anna learned, from her family's experience of war in Europe, the same lesson that Michael Davitt learned in prison: that armed conflict wasn't necessarily the best way to resolve political differences. As she would later point out in her *Tale*, Anna believed that a determined Irish peasantry, standing together in peace 'might, and most likely would' bring about 'a bloodless victory in a few months'.

4

A Respectable Career for Ladies

If the Irish landlords had not deserved extermination for
anything else, they would have deserved it for the treatment
of their own women.

From Anna Parnell, *Tale of a Great Sham*

In the late 1860s, the 'Irish Question' remained a burning issue
– sometimes quite literally. As destitute tenants continued to be
evicted from their homes, their hovels were set on fire, partly as
a warning to others, but mostly to prevent them from quietly
returning when the county sheriff had departed.

The Act of Union in 1800, the removal of a parliament in
Ireland, and the establishment of the Church of Ireland as a
branch of the Church of England, were together the main
catalysts that led to the mass departure of English landlords
back to England. This resulted in the unsatisfactory system of
'absentee landlords' that led to the gradual decline of Ireland's
fortunes. With the landlords at arms length, the threat to their
tenants of eviction for non-payment of rent seemed distant,

but it inevitably led to increased numbers of evictions for non-payment of rent by agents.

These evictions were ultimately counter-productive, because once a tenant was evicted the landlord was likely never to see a penny of the unpaid rent. Also, the legal costs of eviction could soon add up. It was a lose-lose situation for both tenant and landlord.

British Prime Minister Disraeli is described by Anne Power in her text, *Hovels to High Rise – State Housing in Europe since 1850,* as regarding Irish affairs as an onerous but inescapable liability: 'a starving population, an absentee aristocracy, an alien Church, and in addition the weakest executive in the world'. The negative effects of the evictions were not lost on the parliamentarians, who attempted to rectify the situation by disestablishing the Church of Ireland in 1869, and by passing the first Land Reform Act in 1870 to prevent mass evictions for failure to pay rent.

It is into this sad state of affairs, with problem upon problem tracing its roots back to 1800, that the Home Rule movement was to intervene, bringing with it what was claimed to be the solution to the 'Irish Question', by those who knew most about it – the Anglo-Irish landlords who resided there.

Anna was one of the few commentators of the period to point out that there was another layer of impoverishment to the land situation in Ireland. While landlords felt the pressure of their enormous mortgages and raised the rents so high that tenants could not afford to pay them, there was also another group of people who were affected. These were 'quite blameless and helpless', Anna pointed out, and were in fact 'mostly composed of the landlords' female relations, who had annuities secured on landed estates'.

Anna was referring to the female dependents of the land-owning aristocracy, such as widows, unmarried women and the elderly. As income from Irish lands dried up, the landlords stopped paying their women's annuities before cutting their own personal budgets. These dependent women found themselves struggling financially, and so the 'land question' began to evolve into a gender issue, on both sides of the Irish Sea.

Land had been traditionally shared equally among sons and daughters of the farming classes, but 'through the contagion of English ideas' the lands were now being settled mostly on the sons. The result of this 'English idea' of bequeathing land and monies to sons rather than daughters, was that parents left their daughters impoverished unless they found a husband. The situation was worse for dependent Irish ladies than for their English counterparts.

Anna points out that:

English ladies might have only a starvation pittance to live on, but they were not always being threatened with its total extinction, as Irish ladies were, through their male relations destroying the value of the capital … by perpetual rent raising.

It is interesting to note that Anna herself was in this situation, dependent on her family for support, and that she would one day become nearly destitute because of it.

Without a husband or any means to earn an income of their own, all landlords' female relatives were in a difficult situation. Although technically Irish ladies' annuities meant they had a prior claim on the landlords' rental income, these annuities were 'too tiny to permit their taking any legal steps whatever', and landlords – often their brothers or sons – could simply claim in court that they didn't have the money to support their female relatives.

Anna recalled the story of one woman who was forced to sue her own son for payment of the income due to her, but she was defeated in court. Anna knew the family, and stated that 'part of the affidavit by which the [son] gained victory was untrue; but his mother had no power to prove this fact'.

This squeezing of income from female relatives was widely acknowledged, and 'the commiseration extended to them both in England and Ireland was amazing'. In fact, a fund was set up to help them financially, and Distressed Irish Ladies committees were quietly established to provide second-hand clothes and other necessities for women who were affected.

Anna clearly expressed her contempt for this state of affairs, and gave an insight into why she, and her team of ladies, would in the near future, be prepared to risk everything to abolish the system of landlordism in Ireland.

Although Anna was briefly linked with a young clergyman, she had been left destitute by her father and, unable to marry, had to find another way to support herself in a society where a woman's role was increasingly restricted.

During the reign of Queen Victoria, a woman's place was most definitely in the home, and the fashion was to have a home that was furnished and draped with swathes of heavy fabrics. Middle class and aristocratic women's clothing became as heavy and restrictive as the popular furnishings of the day. Dresses became more sexualised – with corsets to thrust breasts upwards and nip in waists, combined with crinoline hoops to make the buttocks and hips appear wider. This emphasis on silhouette was balanced out by the extra layers of fabric to hide as much skin as possible, with long skirts sweeping the floor, necklines to the ears and sleeves covering the wrists and the backs of hands. It was difficult to move freely, and even to breathe properly, causing many women to faint. Indigestion and headaches were also common.

Even housework was almost impossible in these clothes. Housework in the nineteenth century meant hours of hard, physical labour every day. Scrubbing floors, fetching and boiling water, hand-washing heavy fabrics and preparing large meals on a solid fuel stove was very hard work. Everyone who could afford the expense hired at least one servant. Since many households could not afford sufficient servants for all the work, the lady of the house usually wore a day-dress at home, which was a little more comfortable, for light work such as sewing, dusting and polishing.

Working-class women were not subjected to such constraining clothing. Working in a laundry, or as a seamstress, simply wouldn't have been possible in the fashions of the day.

Restricted to their homes by their clothing and the Victorian ideal of domesticity and motherhood, many women found these roles neither as stimulating nor as rewarding as they had been led to believe. For well-read and educated women, the stifling life of a Victorian home was often too much to bear. The ladies began to find creative ways to move out into the community.

Educating the poor on hygiene and domestic virtue was one such acceptable avenue. Popular ladies' literature supported this noble work, and wealthy women all over England and Ireland called into local hovels, bringing home-baked treats and comforting words. These charitable missions, almost imperceptibly, began to build into a grassroots women's movement, extending the female role of service, and eventually emerging as a political force.

In urban England, a young social reformer in her thirties, Octavia Hill (1838–1912), was working with slum-dwellers who she described as 'being as low a class as to have a settled abode'. Her first benefactor was John Ruskin, a renowned art critic, author and founder of the philanthropical trust, the Guild of St George, who gave her the challenge of managing three notorious slum properties in the ironically-named Paradise Place, to see if she could live up to her own aspiration of making 'lives noble, homes happy and family life good'.[1] While public housing policy in Britain was focusing on slum clearance, and knocking down unsafe and unsanitary buildings, Octavia decided that proper management of poor quality, yet habitable, dwellings would improve the lot of the working classes.

Combining social work with housing management, she began her task of improving the slum dwellings, and the tenants themselves. She trained middle class women as managers and rent collectors, and used an authoritarian approach to management. Her work spread from Paradise Place into Freshwater Place and Barrett's Court, and in the course of her career, she took over, restored and managed 15,000 dwellings.

As well as rent collection and basic repairs, Octavia's team of trained volunteers set up meeting halls, savings clubs and even created dramatic productions for general entertainment. Octavia and her team of ladies proved the naysayers wrong when they managed to actually make a small profit from their work, while improving the quality of the housing.

Octavia was careful to place articles about her work in influential magazines, which drew public attention not only to the appalling conditions of the working poor, but also to her groundbreaking methods for overcoming these and improving the quality of life for the residents. These articles were later published as a book, *Homes for the London Poor* (1875), which was so popular that Queen Victoria's daughter, Princess Alice, requested that it be translated into German. Octavia published a further book, *Our Common Land* (1877), calling for open spaces for the urban poor, and went on to become a founder of the National Trust.

In time, Octavia's housing management methods were introduced into Ireland, Holland, Russia and the United States. From small beginnings, Octavia's work grew and was a huge inspiration to others who were seeking a solution to the problem of Britain's growing numbers of urban poor.

Octavia's work was very widely reported and Anna Parnell, as an avid reader, would undoubtedly have heard about her pioneering work methods. Perhaps this was the solution to poverty and evictions in Ireland: a team of middle-class women, working with the poor in their own homes?

In the meantime Anna needed a way to support herself. Art and writing were two of the few respectable careers for an upper middle class lady. Anna's sister Fanny demonstrated a flair for poetry from the age of fifteen, whereas Anna preferred to paint.

CHARLES ELECTED TO PARLIAMENT IN LONDON

In 1874, Anna's brother Charles announced, to the surprise of his entire family, that he would stand for election to the House of Commons as a Home Rule candidate for the county of Wicklow.

Perhaps he had held secret ambitions for some time. He enjoyed being a country landlord, he was interested in politics and was the High Sheriff of Wicklow, and his grandfather had at one point been a candidate for the US presidency. Or perhaps he was simply bored by a life of hunting, fishing and shooting, and disappointed by his one attempt to find a wife. His fiancée, a Miss Woods, whom he had met in Paris, but who had disappeared back to America after he considered himself engaged to her, had damaged his confidence. He had even followed her to America to talk to her in person, but she had refused him.

Whatever the reason, Charles, put his name forward as a future member of parliament. Unfortunately, he discovered that his role as High Sheriff made him ineligible to be elected for

Wicklow. He persuaded his brother John to stand in his place but John was not elected.

Undeterred, Charles stood in a by-election in another county, but was unsuccessful there. His inexperience as a politician, and poor public-speaking skills were probably a factor. Charles, ever the analyst, used this experience to hone his skills on the public platform.

On his third attempt, as a candidate for the county of Meath, Charles was successful – he won with a good majority and finally achieved his goal of becoming a member of parliament. Parnell biographer Côté described how he appeared as he took his seat in the House of Commons on 22 April 1875.

He was then twenty-eight years old and strikingly handsome. He stood over six feet with an upright carriage and slim athletic build. So perfect was the regularity of his facial features – strong jaw, slightly arched nose, high forehead and small, even white teeth – that he would always be a difficult subject for caricaturists. His brown hair, already thinning, a fair, almost blond, beard and a naturally pale complexion set off admirably his wide-spaced brown eyes, remarkable for the intensity of their gaze.

She also described his personality.

He possessed a great personal charm which derived from an air of aloofness, suggesting not arrogance … but a mixture of shyness and proud reserve. The icy composure for which Charles became celebrated could never quite disguise the signs of a tightly reined-in nervous tension – the clenched fist and heightened pallor which appeared at moments of great stress; this hint of the volcano rumbling beneath icy snows proved a powerful attraction to both men and women.

Anna, who moved to London around the same time to continue her art studies, now had the opportunity to observe her brother in action. She was delighted when he was elected as member of parliament for Meath on the Home Rule Party ticket. Charles took his seat in the House of Commons for the first time on 22 April 1875, and witnessed first-hand a dull four-hour speech by Joseph Biggar, whose only purpose seemed to be to slow down the order of business to prevent an unwanted bill from being passed. Charles was fascinated. His party consisted of six elected members of parliament, and here was a way that he could draw the attention of the other six hundred to the issue of Home Rule.

That same year, Anna continued her education at the Heatherly School of Arts. Interested in fine arts, she applied herself diligently to her painting. It was unusual for a woman in her twenties to be still a student, but Anna was encouraged by her mother to live and study in London. The welcome presence of her brother Charles helped to ease any worries Delia may have felt about Anna living so far away from her family. Anna, of course, was more pragmatic and knew that the small annuity left to her by her father, secured on the least profitable of the family's estates, would not be enough to live on once she had completed her education. Her mother Delia was no doubt hopeful that her wilful daughter might find a suitor on campus, or in the social whirl of student life. But Anna, like her father, did not enjoy frivolous social gatherings, and Delia did not really hold out much hope that her plan would succeed. She was resigned in the knowledge that nearly half of all women over twenty-four would remain unmarried. Anna had turned twenty-three that May; spinsterhood beckoned.

In London, Anna was becoming more and more aware of social inequalities between classes and between men and woman. As a young female artist, she was not permitted to sketch nude models, and was thus excluded from applying for a number of scholarships and prizes. She had been frustrated by the limits placed on her freedom in Paris. And she had resented her mother's endeavours to marry her off.

Women in America had much greater freedoms, which even permitted the establishment of a short-lived Fenian Sisterhood in the 1860s.

While living in London, on the outskirts of political life, Anna was acutely aware of how women were excluded from the political process. Herself the victim of poor inheritance laws and tradition, Anna knew that the best way to affect political change was through suffrage, or the right to vote. It could not always be assumed that fathers, husbands or brothers would take proper care of their womenfolk, either financially or in the voting booth. Over the next two years, Anna successfully encouraged her brother Charles to support the right of women to vote.

Married women were considered to be under the legal assumption of 'couverture', that is having no independent existence outside their husbands, as they were 'covered' by his vote. Every other woman was excluded from voting because they were classified, rather unfairly, along with lunatics and criminals, as being incapable of making a rational decision in an election, or holding public office.

It was not that long since universal suffrage for men had been introduced in the UK, after decades of campaigning by the Chartists. The Chartists were a working-class labour movement who had also successfully campaigned for free trade. Their success in obtaining votes for men was quickly followed by the introduction of a broad programme of education. The rationale for introducing education was so to enable the electorate to make informed decisions based on an understanding of history, politics and current affairs, rather than from the dangerous rabble-rousing rhetoric of grumbling dissenters. And of course the British, as with most governments in Europe at the time, were still deeply worried about the prospect of a popular uprising along the lines of the bloody French Revolution.

Education was not therefore seen as being essential for women, as they were not expected to vote. Their husbands, fathers and sons made the electoral decisions for the entire household; an attitude in keeping with the general feeling about the role of women in Victorian times.

CELEBRATING THE CENTENARY OF AMERICAN INDEPENDENCE

No one was more delighted than Charles – except perhaps his mother – when the Home Rule confederation chose him to bring a message of congratulations to the American president on the one-hundredth anniversary of the founding of the American Republic in 1876.

There is a delicious irony to this as well: they had chosen to send Charles, an Anglo-Irish MP of American lineage, and the Fenian MP for Mayo, John O'Connor Power, to congratulate the American people on defeating British rule. This irony would not have been lost on the Parnell family.

There was yet another hidden layer to this congratulatory visit by Charles and his Fenian colleague, indicating that the Home Rule Confederation were not being as forthright in their congratulations as it appeared. First of all, President Grant refused to officially accept their congratulations and simply received them as his guests. This is because protocol demanded that the British ambassador should have presented these congratulations. Second, and more importantly, John O'Connor Power was a Fenian. There had also been two unsuccessful Irish-American Fenian invasions of Canada in both 1867 and 1870, which had caused much tension in the region.

Regardless of the diplomatic ripples caused by his visit, Charles made good use of this opportunity to visit family members in America.

AN UNUSUAL POLITICAL APPRENTICESHIP

By 1877, Anna was still living in London, the proud sister of the member of parliament for Meath. Charles, who was now based in London, but busy commuting between there and

Avondale, was very pleased with the ongoing effectiveness of his party's technique – obstructionism – and Anna couldn't resist the opportunity to watch him in action.

Women were not permitted to sit in the House of Commons since an embarrassing incident in 1778 when a member of parliament, annoyed at seeing a group of ladies taking up seats in the public gallery that his friends wanted to occupy, demanded that they leave. The ladies refused to move, and stubbornly remained there for several hours. Because of this, women were refused entry to the House of Commons for the following fifty years.

However, in 1832, Mrs Elizabeth Fry asked to be permitted to observe a debate about prison discipline, and was escorted to a ventilation space above the ceiling of the chamber where she could watch what was going on from behind the grating.

When the House of Commons was destroyed by fire in 1834, a new gallery was constructed, with a series of openings into the chamber, screened by grilles, but the result of which 'strangely resembled an oriental harem' according to Côté.

This ladies' gallery was dubbed the 'Ladies' Cage', and it was from the vantage point of this strange enclosure that Anna Parnell wrote a series of three articles 'How They Do In The House of Commons: Notes from the Ladies' Cage', which were written in 1877 but published from May to July 1880 in *The Celtic Monthly*.

Rather than record the business of the day, Anna chose instead to observe the effectiveness of the political process, which she wrote about in the impersonal manner of a detached third person. What she learned was to challenge her ideas about the usefulness of campaigning for political change. Charles had told her about obstructionism and she was fully prepared.

Anna was pleased to note that slowing down the process of legislation by tediously long arguments achieved its purpose. She noted that:

> The greatest sufferers by it [obstructionism] were the attendants of the House, who were not sufficiently numerous to allow division into relays, and were consequently obliged to keep awake, as best they might, the whole night. The Sergeant-at-Arms, a charming, white-haired old gentleman, was so much exhausted, that he set fire to himself that evening by falling asleep over his post-prandial cigar, but happily without any damage.

The House grew cold at night during the endless debates, and MPs put on their coats to keep warm. One footman, on seeing that his master's coat was gone from his peg, presumed that his master had gone home. Another unnamed MP was so traumatised after a forty-two-hour parliamentary debate in the freezing cold that he disappeared, and was found a week later by his distressed wife, in a hotel room, where he had been trying to recover.

Reflecting on this, Anna commented that the Ladies' Cage was in fact a blessing, because the ladies had 'considerable advantages which were denied to the men – freedom to stand up, to talk, to keep their hats on and above all, freedom to go to sleep'.

Obstructionism was, however, an effective tactic, as Beverly Schneller reports: 'the observers were much more interested in keeping the Home Rule Party from participating in the debates than in debating the measures at hand.'[2] The opposition was portrayed as 'unfocused, easily distracted, vindictive' and 'cranky' according to Schneller.

Feelings in the House were occasionally 'bordering on hysteria', for example when, during a long drawn-out debate about the South Africa Bill which Charles' party had obstructed.[3] Charles was ejected from the House at the insistence of an infuriated Sir Stafford Northcote. Northcote accused Charles of making treasonous remarks by suggesting that 'it had always been the custom of the English to ill-use and oppress those races which fell under their rule and that, he as an Irishman, felt it in his interest to thwart the intentions of the government'.

While the government debated whether Charles should be permitted to return or arrested for treason, he took the opportunity to join his sister Anna in the Ladies' Cage. Like co-conspirators, they observed the proceedings against him. In some sense being forced to join the women was perhaps intended to emasculate him, but this did not seem to bother Charles. He had chosen voluntarily to join his sister, who would no doubt have been delighted to be thus complicit in a parliamentary revolt. The irony of the situation was not lost on either of them. Being banished to the Ladies' Cage, rather than being a method of exclusion, was now one of the best vantage points in the House.

A debate ensued, during which it was observed that Charles had not said anything that subjects from other colonies had not said in the past, and therefore his words could not be considered treason. It was also pointed out, quite sensibly, that if people were not permitted to speak out against the government in the House of Commons, this would have the overall effect of forbidding any kind of debate at all, and then 'what would become of Her Majesty's loyal opposition?' Lord Harrington suggested that they mull over this conundrum for a week, and in the meantime Charles was permitted to return to the chamber.

A delighted Anna noted that 'poor Sir Stafford Northcote was obliged to put his thunderbolt back into his pocket and watch the enemy walking up to his seat and hear him go on with his speech just where he had left off'. To make matters worse, Charles continued obstructing the meeting, and the sitting continued until five o'clock in the morning.

Anna reported that the next day 'the motion to suspend the member for Meath was quietly discharged'. This embarrassing quarrel between Parnell and Northcote resulted in two new House rules which limited the number of adjournments that could be called and forbade the Speaker from throwing a member out of a debate unless the member was voted out of order by a vote of the entire House. Charles had won.

The Home Rule Party achieved a number of notable results from their campaign of obstructionism. All remaining Fenian prisoners were released in 1877, including Michael Davitt, who was soon to play an important role in Anna's political formation, and who would become her strongest supporter.

Anna's hand was clearly visible in Charles' support of the motion to include girls in the 1878 Irish Intermediate Education

Act; this was an essential first step in obtaining votes for women. The barbaric practice of flogging as a means of military discipline, while it would not be abolished completely until 1879 on the grounds that it was as important as 'the Speaker's wig or the Sergeant's sword', was halved in severity from fifty lashes to twenty-five. This may seem a small, unconnected victory for a political party who wanted to achieve political independence for Ireland, but it demonstrates compassion for the sufferings inflicted on the lower ranks of the military, and an abhorrence of violence.

By the end of the parliamentary session, the presence of this tiny party of six members had been well and truly felt. Home Rule was finally about to find a place on the agenda.

5

Poverty and the Fenians
in Post-Famine Ireland

In the first half of the nineteenth century, there was widespread poverty throughout Europe. England, still mostly rural, faced many of the same problems as Ireland. England was 'saved' economically to some extent by industrialisation but the majority of the population was still living in the countryside.

In many ways, England was just as much a developing country as Ireland, although urban poverty was greater in England, and rural poverty greater in Ireland. The solutions that worked in England could not work in Ireland, as the two sets of problems were entirely different.

Public health became a government issue in the 1840s in England, with the passing of the first Public Health Act in 1848. The death in 1861 of Queen Victoria's husband Prince Albert from cholera, a preventable waterborne disease, brought public health to the top of the political agenda.

Public health problems were inextricably linked to poor quality housing for the urban working classes in particular. Contaminated drinking water supplies and poor sewerage infrastructure quite literally spilled over into the safe havens of the middle and upper classes. This was not a problem in rural areas, which did not suffer from the same problems of overcrowding and having nowhere to dispose of sewage and household waste.

Individuals were powerless to tackle the public health issue, but still the state was unwilling to intervene. Slum clearance legislation was a first step, although it had the unfortunate side effect of moving the impoverished occupants of these tenements into already overcrowded buildings nearby.

Private enterprise was seen as the Victorian solution to the problem. Octavia Hill had proved that efficient management could improve not only the profitability, but also the quality, of housing for the urban poor, and this made it attractive for new landlords. Encouraged by the state, semi-charitable efforts were made to tackle the problem. A new concept known as 'philanthropy at five percent' began to rise in popularity.[1] Investors, who could easily make profits of ten percent elsewhere, invested money in housing projects with the understanding that they would only make a five per cent profit. This was in line with negative Victorian thinking about 'charity', which was deemed to make poor people dependent on handouts rather than encouraging them to take the initiative to earn their own incomes.

Businesses such as the Improved Industrial Dwellings Company were set up by entrepreneurs and in support of this, the state passed legislation such as the Labouring Classes' Dwelling Houses Act of 1866, which allowed semi-charitable companies to borrow money from the Public Works Loan Commissioners. Despite all of these initiatives, however, the rents were still too high for most of the urban poor. Only those with the best incomes, who were reasonably well-housed already, could afford to live in the quality housing. While ploughing ahead with investment and financial strategies, these noble entrepreneurs had overlooked the fact that Octavia Hill's army of highly trained women managers were working as volunteers.

Wealthy capitalists, whose own riches were built upon the labour of the poor, were conscious of the plight of those who had worked so hard but who had so little to show for it. Charitable housing trusts were set up by benefactors such as Guinness, Peabody and Rothschild to address the situation. In 1862, for example, the Peabody Trust was established with an endowment of £150,000 to provide housing for the working classes. These strategies had limited success, again partly due to the relatively high costs of the rent, and a desire to avoid overcrowding. The strictly authoritarian housing management strategies and zero tolerance of rent arrears, made these dwellings less popular than they might otherwise have been.

This emphasis on public health and housing for the urban poor in England meant that Ireland's problems – which were entirely different – were more difficult for the state legislature to comprehend, and therefore slower to be tackled.

As a result of urbanisation caused by industrialisation, and the public health issues inherent in housing these new urban working classes, there were a number of hard-working charities in existence to look after their needs. As an elected representative, the lord mayor of every city was expected to ensure the Poor Law was adhered to, and to assist with other charitable work. One example of such a charity was the Sick & Indigent Roomkeepers' Society, established in 1790 by a group of Dublin merchants.

From the late eighteenth century onwards, Dublin slum-dwellers, in common with their English counterparts, often lived crowded together in one room, often more than one family sharing the room, or at least one lodger to help with the rent. The demand for accommodation in the city, and the lack of supply, meant that rents were enormous.

The Society provided basic relief, such as fuel and potatoes to the very poorest. Within three years, they had created four divisions which covered the city. By 1855, the Society moved to a new building on Palace Street, off Dame Street, right next to Dublin Castle. And although by this stage many of the wealthy elite had abandoned their Georgian houses and sought refuge in the country, the Society still managed to generate enough income to continue their work.

However, Anna was particularly concerned for the rural poor. Whereas in England, poverty was worst in towns and cities, it was the opposite in Ireland. Ireland's fresh, flowing streams, her lakes teaming with fish, fertile green pastures and open air were considered to be the healthiest of environments in which to live. Ireland had recovered well from the famine in the 1840s, and was starting to enjoy 'a little more comfort', as Anna Parnell put it. She elaborated by saying that 'tenant farmers, for instance, had, many of them, got into the extravagant habit of drinking tea twice a day'. Remittances were being sent regularly from Irish emigrants in America, and even the constant rent increases from absentee landlords were not a major problem. By the late 1870s, Ireland appeared to be flourishing, and the term 'prosperity' was beginning to be cautiously used to describe her economy.

But in 1878, emigrants began to return to Ireland from America, due to the downturn of the American economy. Perhaps Irish people were painting a far better picture of life than was the actual case, or perhaps the emigrants were homesick, but Anna Parnell said that 'this return of emigrants was probably caused by the increase of "hard times" in the United States [more] than by improvement in Ireland'.

AN INTERNATIONAL FOOD CRISIS CAUSED BY GLOBALISATION

It was successful mechanised agricultural practices in America that precipitated a food crisis in England, Ireland, Scotland and Wales in the late 1870s. With huge swathes of land under intense crop production in the United States, and bumper harvests, the price of grain had fallen considerably in world markets. Tenant farmers throughout Great Britain and Ireland were particularly badly affected as grains imported from the Americas flooded the local market. Overnight, the value of their crops plummeted, while in Ireland the rents continued to increase.

For many years, the rents for England's farms were kept artificially low, thanks to government policy. This was good news for the tenant farmers, but bad news for the landlords. However, rents in Ireland were not capped, and lands in Ireland became highly prized for this very reason – with rents rising in Ireland, and a tenant class willing to pay these increases, landlords took full advantage of the situation.

Anna wrote in her *Tale* that 'certain big landlords, with seats in the House of Lords, who had land in both countries ... might naturally be anxious to make their Irish tenants pay for the losses they had to sustain in England. Letting themselves be led by this class of people has spread ruin amongst Irish landlords; I think it has done a good deal of damage to the English Squirarchy as well.'

But even though rents in England were lower, Anna Parnell conceded that:

> English farmers, it must be remembered, had also suffered through the fall in agricultural prices ... though their rents had not been previously screwed up to the highest point, as Irish rents had been.
>
> Before the year 1879, landlords had always taken it for granted that rents must always tend to increase, as by some fixed law of the universe, and had regarded themselves as having the power to command at any time they liked an increased income by raising their rents.

This in effect was true. Often living beyond their means,

landowners with portfolios of property in England and Ireland had only one option to increase their income, and that was to increase their rents in Ireland. At the same time, political focus in the British parliament was on keeping rents low for tenant farmers in England, that they might produce sufficient food for the labouring classes in the cities and in this way increase overall prosperity. And it was working – Great Britain was, at that time, the wealthiest kingdom in the world, although this wealth was very unevenly distributed amongst its subjects, many of whom lived in abject poverty.

As Anna put it:

> … the whole energy of parliament [was] employed in keeping up the incomes of landlords in Ireland, while those in England were expected to reduce theirs voluntarily, and make no fuss about it.

She also felt that although this was grossly unfair to Irish tenants, it had the unexpected side-effect of reducing the power of landlords, a fact that was soon to be used against them in the Land War. She clarified this by explaining how this weakened the landlord class:

> This fancied security of always being in a position to gain and never to lose without even having to work for the gain, had the inevitable consequence of breeding an utterly worthless and helpless set of men.

Having identified the weaknesses of the absentee landlord

system, Anna knew that when the time was right to tackle the 'Irish Question' these weaknesses could be capitalised on to full advantage.

MICHAEL DAVITT AND THE FENIANS

Anna Parnell's life soon changed when, through her brother Charles' political connections, she met the dashing one-armed Fenian, Michael Davitt. Michael had been released a few months previously from prison, where he was in the eighth year of a fifteen-year sentence for suspected gun-running. While in prison, Davitt smuggled out letters describing the inhumane conditions in which prisoners were held. Côté posits that 'the moral courage of a man prepared to face the inevitable consequences of defying prison authorities to obtain fair treatment for the most despised layer of society appealed to Anna's sense of humanity and justice'.

In 1877, thanks to the work of the Home Rulers and Charles Stewart Parnell witnessed by Anna from the Ladies' Cage, political prisoners were re-classified as 'first class mis-demeanants', rather than as felons who were convicted as murderers and common criminals. Michael Davitt was released that December on parole. Côté continues 'this young man, then thirty-one years old, was to play a major role in the land agitation and, both directly and indirectly, in Anna's life'.

Like Anna, Davitt had no memory of the famine of the 1840s. His family had emigrated to England when he was around three years old. At the tender age of nine, in common with most working class families of the time, the young Michael was sent to work in a cotton factory. Conditions in factories were notoriously dangerous. Although the first Cotton Mills and Factories Act had been passed in 1819 to regulate the conditions of child workers in these factories, and an act known as the 'Ten Hours Act', limiting the hours of young persons and females in factories to no more than ten hours per day had also been introduced in 1847, there were few factory inspectors, and they had limited powers of enforcement. By 1878 there had been no fewer than eight acts of parliament regulating employment in cotton mills and factories, but conditions remained as dangerous as before.

At around the age of eleven, Michael Davitt lost his right arm in an industrial accident. A bright young boy, his local parish priest saw his potential and arranged that he be sent to school. Côté says that:

> Raised among the exiled and despised Irish of the north of England and fed on harrowing tales of suffering and oppression from the Famine victims themselves, Davitt became imbued with a hatred of landlordism and British rule in Ireland.
>
> Davitt's darkly handsome good looks and the empty sleeve, mute testimony to a life of early privation, made him a romantic figure on the public platform.

Upon his release in 1877, Davitt's first impulse was to visit his family in America, who had all moved there from England while he had been in prison. He went in May 1878. Although he had discovered pacifism while in prison, he was still perceived as a committed Fenian, and when he arrived in America he discovered that the Clan na Gael (an American branch of the Fenians) had organised a lecture tour for him across America.

The Fenian movement was struggling at that time. For many years they had waited for just the right time for armed insurrection in Ireland, but the perfect time had never come. Frustrated Fenians in exile in America had attempted other ways to attack England, such as planning an invasion of the vast country of Canada. As Côté so eloquently puts it:

> After years of false starts and rumours, recruiting campaigns and squabbling within the leadership, all duly reported by spies to the British Embassy in Washington and to the Canadian Minister of Justice in Ottawa, a 'vast army of 400' Fenians had crossed the Manitoba border and held a small fort for ten hours before being rounded up and captured.

The Fenian movement in America was in tatters; humiliated, defeated and accused of misappropriating funds raised for their cause. They were depending on the imposing figure of Michael Davitt to rekindle their revolutionary spirit and fight once again for Ireland.

They were to be disappointed, because Davitt was keen to promote what he called 'a new departure', a concept he had learned from John Devoy, one of the leading American Fenians of the time. This new approach – which essentially meant abandoning military action – considered that a combination of parliamentary action and the collective action of Irish tenant farmers would lead to an independent Ireland and full ownership of the land.

Davitt recognised that armed uprisings against a vastly superior enemy would not achieve the Fenians' aims. Tenant farmers in the west of Ireland were already forming themselves into tenants rights associations, calling for fair rents and to protect themselves from evictions. He recognised in Charles Stewart Parnell a leader who could mediate between the two extremes of land reform – those who wanted a political settlement, and those who preferred a more militant approach. From November onwards, Davitt spoke warmly about Charles' political work. The more militant Fenian leaders were disappointed that Davitt's speaking tour didn't generate the expected rush of recruits willing to fight to the death for Irish freedom. Davitt's legacy in America was a greater understanding of the needs of the Irish people, and a moderate approach to land reform and self-determination.

When Davitt returned from America, he became involved in organising the first mass meeting of tenant farmers in Irishtown, County Mayo. He was committed to peaceful means to resolve the Land War and he understood that this needed the support of every farmer in Ireland.

6

A New Leadership Emerges

After a hard winter and a year of biting winds, icy rain and wild storms in the west, and damp, miserable weather in the rest of the country, the harvests of 1879 were looking bad. Tenant farmers were deeply in debt to banks and shopkeepers, and 'gale day' was rapidly approaching, the day when the twice-annual rent had to be paid. The numbers of evictions were already rising and it looked like the country was again facing a real threat of famine.

Activists across the country were deciding what to do to avoid a repetition of the disaster of the 1840s. Once again, peasants had just enough money to either pay the rent or feed themselves. But this time, tenants no longer believed that paying their rent was the most prudent thing to do. The failures of all the strategies of the 1840s lived on in people's memories. This time a different approach was needed.

Even while policy-makers were convening meetings and discussing the political merits of various options, the tenants were considering theirs; whether to risk paying the rent and risk dying of starvation, or whether to withhold the rent and risk eviction. Eviction in winter could also be a death sentence, through exposure, hunger or disease. But withholding the rent gave tenants a last, desperate respite, and if the end result was to be the same, then perhaps it was the lesser of two evils. As Anna pointed out:

> There were four ways in which landlords could proceed against non-paying tenants – eviction, sale of the tenants' interest in the county court (which had to be followed by eviction to be made effective), distraint of goods and stock, and action in the bankruptcy court.

Bankruptcy proceedings were costly, time-consuming and ultimately pointless, so landlords seldom bothered with that option. The first two options, eviction, and sale of the tenancy followed by eviction, were similar, but troublesome. Even after all the bother of an eviction, a tenant had the right under law within six months of the eviction to repay his debts and move back in, known as the 'six months redemption'.

Lurking in the background were the hated 'land grabbers': landless or tenant farmers, who were only too delighted to take over a farm when a family was evicted. The shortage of farmland and a steady growth in population, meant that this was an all too common occurrence.

Despite the fact that most farms in Ireland were worked by tenant farmers, those tenants did in fact have a certain level of security of tenure, that is, the right to remain on their land under the terms of a lease. Leases could be made for a person's lifetime, meaning that until the person concerned died the landlord could not evict the tenant from the land and rent it to someone else.

Distraint, or removing goods and stock such as furniture and cattle and selling them to cover the unpaid rent, was on the face of it a much simpler option. But the destitution of the tenants meant that this option was seldom used, for often there was nothing worth taking. Anna describes in her *Tale* one story of a landlord who removed a tenant's goods in lieu of rent:

> I have only once heard of a landlord annexing any of a tenant's furniture; this was a Mayo landlord, named Walter Bourke, who was High Sheriff for the county, and used to do his own evicting by virtue of his office. I was told he had once taken the best of two blankets he found in a tenant's hovel. This man was eventually shot, together with the soldier who was protecting him. I believe he was the last landlord shot in Ireland.

Being shot for taking a blanket is an extreme example, but landlords had other options as well. Distraint could be used to remove crops from a field – difficult, but not impossible. This was made simpler if the tenant had already taken the trouble to harvest them. Removing these crops to a market to sell them was more problematic, the difficulty being that local people were not keen to purchase crops taken in this way. This resulted in the landlords having the costly and time-consuming task of transporting the crops to other markets to sell them. These goods were at risk of theft, too, and it was necessary to hire a guard to protect them.

However, livestock was a different story. Cattle, for instance, could be herded; they didn't require a horse and wagon for transportation. Tenants had a number of ways to prevent their cattle being taken. Cattle could only be taken if they were out in the fields, so the tenants could keep them in the byre during the day and let them out to graze at night when it was almost impossible to round them up, or they could herd them back into the byre during the day if they knew the landlord was coming. Even if they did manage to take some of the cattle, landlords often found that they were unable to get a good price for them in the open market.

Frustrated landlords had to come up with another solution, which they did. As Anna Parnell pointed out: 'The laws of cruelty to animals could not be carried out against the allies of the government.' In practice, this meant that landlords would take tenants' cattle and then openly mistreat them. This was an effective way of encouraging tenants to pay their rent. 'Overstocking' or cramming too many cattle into too small a space was a common way in which landlords did this. The tenants, appalled by this treatment of their animals, would do everything they could to buy the cattle back.

Around this time, remittances from America were starting to dry up. The economic downturn there was starting to bite, and the thousands of Irish emigrants who had worked as navvies building the great American railways were finding it harder to get work. Stories of the beginnings of prosperity in Ireland saw the beginnings of a return to the homeland. Anna Parnell reported that as early as 1878, 'Captains of Atlantic liners said there were as many emigrants going one way as the other.'

Meanwhile, in England and Scotland there was a series of disastrous harvests. The years 1873, 1875, 1876 and 1879 were bad, but the very worst harvest of the century was in 1879. The unfavourable weather was a disaster for farmers. There were severe outbreaks of blight, mould and mildew in fruits, vegetables, potatoes and grains. Livestock suffered from pleuro-pneumonia, 'liver-rot' and foot-and-mouth disease. Almost 70 per cent of the grain consumed had to be imported. Although consumers were grateful for this bountiful supply of imported wheat from America, it had the effect of reducing the price indigenous farmers could obtain for their own produce. Because of a flood of cheap imported grain, English grain prices stayed artificially low, when in normal circumstances a shortage of home-grown produce would have led to an increase in prices for farmers. British agriculture was already four years into a depression, which lasted until the end of the century.

Falling grain prices led to a reduction in profits and farmers struggled to pay the rents for their land. The unprofitability of farming led to many more rural dwellers moving to the cities in search of paid employment. Large areas of land remained fallow, and landlords found it hard to attract new tenants. Rents plummeted, to little effect. Productivity dropped in farms that continued to operate. And all the while, foreign imports continued to keep the price of domestic produce down. Farmers who had invested in developing their lands during times of prosperity now saw their investments literally rotting in the ground.

It was generally perceived that the sunless, rainy weather of the 1870s had almost destroyed British agriculture, and commentators of the day described the situation as a 'general calamity'. Joseph Arch, a radical activist for rural workers' rights, was the president of the National Agricultural Labourers' Union with over 86,000 members – over one-tenth of all farm workers in England. He commented that people who were still working to maximise production on their farms were only doing so to save enough money to give up farming for good. 'For the last twenty-five years,' he said, 'farmers have farmed to leave instead of farmed to stay.' Across England, farmers began to sink into debt as they purchased food on credit from shopkeepers, and borrowed money from the banks.

Thousands of Irish peasants arrived in England, desperate for work. Katharine O'Shea commented in her memoir that:

> Irish hop-pickers were so inured to privation in their own country that they were very popular among the Kentish hop-farmers, as they did not grumble so much as did the English pickers at the scandalously inefficient accommodation provided them.

A Royal Commission was appointed in 1879 to investigate what was happening and why. The commission mostly blamed the weather, but of course the bad weather did not explain why the price of farm produce had fallen instead of risen, which it should have done as demand outstripped supply. A second commission was set up to look at the effects of the globalisation of food production, focusing on meat and wheat.

Ironically, it was the Irish navvies who had left Ireland and worked to construct the railways who had opened up the American mid west with its fertile, virgin soil. In these ideal conditions, crops had flourished. The improvement of transcontinental and transatlantic transportation also meant that America was linked to England, Ireland and Continental Europe by rail and by sea. Competing merchant fleets haggled over freight contracts, driving down the price of transportation.

And it was not long before other countries like Australia, New Zealand and Argentina were exporting their produce to Europe. Unable to compete on grain production, many British farmers turned instead to dairy farming, and arable land was converted to pasture across the country. But this too began to be affected by imports.

Squeezed on all sides by superior, or at least vastly cheaper food imports, Britain realised it was unable to compete. However, as an industrial state, Britain was still a leader, with a large export trade in manufactured goods. Britain simply stopped trying to be a food-producing nation, and focused instead on manufacturing.

A NEW LEADERSHIP EMERGES IN IRELAND

In December 1878, Michael Davitt had returned to Ireland, and in the early months of 1879 he was organising mass meetings of tenants who had suffered the effects of the recent poor harvest.

The first of these meetings was in Irishtown, County Mayo, where tenant farmers called for rent reductions and demanded an end to evictions for rent arrears. Michael Davitt was the main organiser, but did not speak at the meeting. Charles Stewart Parnell was also conspicuous by his absence. Perhaps they did not attend because they were carefully assessing how this activist approach would be perceived by the authorities. This first mass meeting was a huge success.

Unable to stand on the sidelines any more, Charles Stewart Parnell travelled to Westport, County Mayo in early June 1879 to join Michael Davitt and spoke for the first time at a public meeting. His only speech that summer contained the nascent ideologies of what soon became known as 'the Land War': that tenants should have the right to purchase their own lands, that they should not pay unfair rents at a time when famine threatened, and that they should do all they could to stay in their homesteads. Whether this was a plea to the people not to emigrate was unclear, but since it was often the healthiest and strongest workers who had left in the past, it was definitely intended to encourage the strong to stand beside the weak. Charles Stewart Parnell, ever the astute politician, encouraged tenants to do all these things but only 'if without injuring the landlord'. There may have been many activists who were willing to stir up agitation in the countryside, but he was not one of them.

Throughout the remainder of the damp and miserable summer of 1879, Michael Davitt held many similar meetings throughout Connaught, accompanied by other land reform activists such James Daly and James Bryce Killen. Conscious of the need for Irish-American support, these meetings were all carefully noted and reported in the Irish-American press.

In the early autumn of that year, Charles Stewart Parnell joined them. 'Gale day' was fast approaching in November, the day on which the next tranche of rents were due, and it was important to rally enough support to have a real impact. Word of mouth was not sufficient, and newspapers were not widely read enough to have real impact; getting out there and talking to the masses was the only way to spread ideas.

The effects were felt quite quickly. When word spread, some landlords cautiously offered reductions in the rents; perhaps especially those landlords who had holdings in Britain and who knew that Irish rents were unfair by comparison. With tenant farmers abandoning the land in droves in Britain and the profitability of farming plummeting, the last thing landlords with Irish estates needed was for the same thing to happen in Ireland. Irish tenants probably didn't know about what was happening in Britain and saw this as a capitulation by the landlords, so word spread about the effectiveness of noisy agitation.

During this time, the harvests came in. The harvest was the worst since the 1840s in Ireland, and the worst ever in Britain. Famine seemed inevitable unless tenants continued to stand together and work in unison for an equitable solution to the problem of excessively high rents.

ANNA IN AMERICA

Before the miserable Irish winter of 1878 had fully set in, Anna had travelled to America to join her mother and younger sisters in Bordentown, New Jersey, and stayed there until the summer of 1880 for an extended visit. The family followed the newspaper reports about Ireland with interest. It was not all good news; the opposing view to the popular demonstrations was that withholding rent was a form of theft and that the gentlemen were spreading a malicious form of communism designed to overthrow the landlords. The daily papers in New York printed short rebuttals to the tenants' claims of unfair rents, which were supplied by correspondents in Dublin who took the 'side' of the landlords. Cartoons, depicting the rural Irish as savage 'boghoppers', were published in Britain, in an attempt to undermine the credibility of the movement and its leaders.

In mid-November, Davitt, Daly and Killen were all arrested for the crime of sedition, because Davitt had said at a public meeting that it was time that the men of Ireland stood up to the landlords. The *New York Tribune* published an article claiming that the fair rent movement was in fact turning militant and was calling for landlords to be shot.

Anna and Fanny both wrote to the offending newspaper. While Fanny wrote an emotional note claiming the article was libellous, Anna with her customary cool objectivity wrote that rather than inciting murder, some of her brother's speeches were instead 'occasionally interrupted by exclamations of homicidal tendency' and that 'his audiences have now ceased to offer these objectionable suggestions'. Anna remarked that it was just as well Davitt hadn't also called for the womanhood of Ireland to stand up, or 'he would have been tried for high treason'. Her letter continued the argument that rather than the Land League being the ones who were threatening violence and shootings, the reverse was true, but with a more obtuse weapon. 'Why is it murder to kill a few men with powder and ball,' she said, 'and not murder to kill hundreds and thousands of men, women and children by cold and hunger?'

Charles used the media interest to launch an international press campaign calling for the release of 'The Gurteen Three'.[1] A series of mass meetings was held in Ireland to protest at the arrests, and the case against the three men collapsed. This was Charles' and Anna's first real taste of victory; the government were seen to back down when faced with public protests and media outrage.

After this, the *New York Tribune* printed no more articles condemning the Land League, but instead printed a supportive editorial the following week and sent a journalist, James Redpath, to Ireland to find out the true story. Côté said that all the journalists who were sent from America and other countries to report on the issue became 'ardent advocates for the Irish Land League and bitterly hostile critics of the landlords. This was an encouraging step for the sisters and they began to consider other means by which they might publicise the League.'

Anna and Fanny were delighted to hear that Charles would soon travel to America to raise funds for the Land League, but the *New York Herald* was not. An article claimed that any funds raised for the cause would be 'misappropriated'. This was not an entirely fabricated suggestion, as Côté remarks:

> ... there were also the Fenian disturbances to stir the pot of anti-Irish feelings and the strange propensity for funds subscribed for Irish purposes to disappear without account.

The Irish cause always had a difficult time with the press, because the British reports of Irish people often matched the caricature that the Irish were 'a troublesome, quarrelling and feckless lot'. Côté continues 'memories of the swarms of ragged, fever-carrying Famine immigrants who had filled the charity hospitals and poorhouses lingered as an impression of an unclean group. Bridget, the serving maid of Boston, and Paddy, the rough labourer or cartman, were bywords for slovenly incompetence.'

Côté also reports that 'the houses of prostitution from Montreal to New Orleans were stocked with illiterate Irish girls for, as Archbishop Lynch of Toronto had pointed out in 1864, the Irish were the only national group that allowed untrained and illiterate girls to go off alone to a distant land where they fell "not easy victims but after much struggle" to the brothel-keepers and madams of the great cities.'

This concern with the moral welfare of women who had suffered from eviction in Ireland, or who had chosen to emigrate because of the threat of eviction, was one of the reasons that the clergy – both Catholic and Church of Ireland – were keen to prevent landlords from evicting tenants.

The British parliament was struggling to cope with what appeared to be the imminent collapse of British agriculture. When rumours reached the House of Commons of a possible famine in Ireland as well, there were fears of further disaster in both economic and human terms.

Information on the situation in Ireland was delivered to the British parliament via a rather biased source. James Lowther

(1840-1904) had been appointed under-secretary of state for the colonies in 1874, and became the chief secretary for Ireland in 1878. This was somewhat unfortunate, both for Lowther and the Land League, as he had been vehemently opposed to the Land Bill. However, in his role as chief secretary, he was asked to report to parliament about the rumours of impending famine in Ireland. He reported that there was 'no notable distress in Ireland', and the parliament heaved a sigh of relief. If Anna had seen Lowther's report, she would no doubt have been furious.

Anna was not without compassion for the plight of farmers in England, and conceded that the British government had to deal with similar problems at home. 'English farmers, it must be remembered, had also suffered through the fall in agricultural prices', she said, 'though their rents have not been previously screwed up to the highest point, as Irish rents had been.' The fall in grain prices, and the poor harvest, was therefore affecting Irish tenant farmers much harder than their counterparts in England, a fact that seemed lost on Ireland's chief secretary.

THE IRISH NATIONAL LAND LEAGUE

The minor successes in rent reductions in the west of Ireland, combined with huge public support and a growing need for a structure to control this new mass movement led to the establishment of the Irish National Land League on 21 October 1879 in Dublin. Anna later wrote in her *Tale* about the main aims of the League, beginning with collective bargaining to reduce rents, by withholding payment until a fair rent could be agreed:

> Its [the Land League's] ultimate aim was the conversion of the tenants into the owners of their holdings … [tenants] were also told that no tenants should make a separate settlement for himself, however satisfactory it might be, unless all the others were included, even those who might have nothing to offer, the richer tenants thus protecting the poorer.

Charles Stewart Parnell was elected president of the new League, and Michael Davitt became its secretary. For the first time, the tenant farmers of Ireland had a leadership that combined popular mass civil action with a voice in the parliament in Westminster.

The first order of business was to prevent evictions, by supporting tenants associations in collective actions to negotiate fair rents, and the second was to enable tenants to purchase their holdings. This work clearly required a lot of money and the obvious place to get this money was from the displaced Irish now living in America. The recent speaking tours by Michael Davitt had shown the level of support that was already there. Although there was little heart for supporting a Fenian-style armed insurrection, a more moderate approach could gain the financial and moral support of the vast majority of exiled Irish.

Fanny paved the way for Charles' tour of America with her

article *The Irish Land Question* published in the *North American Review*, which was compiled using the text of his speeches over the previous eight months. In it, she compared the situation of the rural poor in Ireland to other countries in Europe such as the Netherlands, Italy, France and Belgium.

The article argued that the reason tenants in Ireland had been prepared to pay high rents was not because of the profitability of the land, but its scarcity. Absentee landlords, learning from the experience of the falling value of grains on their own land in England, had begun moving to livestock husbandry. The most fertile lands in the plains of Ireland were being systematically converted to dairy farming. Firstly, the smaller tenants were systematically removed from the land, then it was levelled and grasslands and pasture suitable for grazing were sown. As a consequence, the evicted tenants were being forced to farm poorer lands further up the valleys. It was therefore scarcity, rather than quality, which drove rents higher.

The article was also designed to explain how the work of the Land League was acting to quell the threat of violence in Ireland. Fanny argued that by collectively negotiating for rent reductions and explaining the situation to their landlords, the tenants were in fact preventing a violent uprising in Ireland that could occur if evictions proceeded *en masse*. Without a reasoned political solution, the desperate poor could feel there was no option but a violent uprising. The Land League, she argued, was the calm and rational solution to this. The article was published under her brother's name.

THE NUN OF KENMARE

In the heart of a Poor Clare convent in Kenmare, County Kerry, one of the first places to be affected by the threat of famine, a cloistered nun called Sr Mary Frances Clare decided to take immediate action to feed the hungry. A superb letter writer, with correspondence regularly appearing in newspapers in England, Ireland, America, Canada and Australia, she knew exactly what to do.

Using a technique which is still the backbone of charity direct mail fundraising today, Sr Mary Frances sent letters in October 1879 to everyone on her substantial mailing lists describing the horrific suffering of the poor and asking for donations.

She also knew that to keep her donors happy, proper acknowledgement was important, so when the donations were received, they were carefully listed in a pamphlet that was published quarterly and sent to supporters. Sr Mary Frances was an astute woman: as well as helping the poor and needy in surrounding parishes through the local Catholic clergy and religious, she also sent money to Protestant ministers. The icing on the cake for donors was the promise that the nuns would pray for their deceased loved ones and personal favours, known as 'special intentions'.

In November 1879, Famine Fund collection boxes appeared in post offices all over America. This was the work of Fanny Parnell on behalf of Sr Mary Frances. Although this was a departure from her work with the main Land League, and possibly in competition with the League's own activities, it was certainly a way of channelling funding to a local initiative where it could have most impact.

Sr Mary Frances Clare's collection was to be the first fund-raising activity of four competing funds, and Fanny and Anna learned a lot about effective fundraising by supporting her.

As Fanny and Anna campaigned in the United States, tenant farmers in Ireland were demanding either fair rent, or to buy their own land, both of which were technically possible, but still financially unfeasible.

A system of fair rents had already been set up in the 1850s and 1860s, in response to the charge of unfair rents leading to the famine of the 1840s. A commissioner of valuation, Sir Richard Griffith, had been sent to Ireland in 1852, the year Anna Parnell was born, to set reasonable rents for Irish farmland based on a rateable valuation. His work continued until 1865, although upon the conclusion of the valuation most landlords simply used his findings as a base point for rents and increased them year on year based on supply and demand – that is, if a tenant was prepared to pay a higher rent on the open market, then that higher rent became the new rent. In 1879, many tenants associations called for the 'Griffith's valuation' to be reintroduced as the fairest approximation of a fair rent. This was indeed a reasonable request, given that rents for farmland in England was plummeting.

In addition to the commission to set fair rents in Ireland, the British government eventually yielded to Irish farmers' requests for a process to purchase their holdings. The House of Commons, the House of Lords and Queen Victoria herself heard and understood the claims that the famine of the 1840s was caused in part by pro-landlord legislation. In 1870, five years after Griffith's extensive valuation work, the legislature passed into law the first Land Reform Act for Ireland. This law included a number of clauses, dubbed the 'Bright Clauses', which enabled tenants to purchase their land.[2]

The law included the surprising concession of a loan at reasonable interest rates from the British government itself. However, like much legislation in the nineteenth century, it was permissive rather than enabling and the conditions required to actually purchase the land were prohibitive. A tenant must first make a down payment of one-third of the cost of the land, and then the balance could be financed with the loan. Saving up a one-third down payment was impossible for the vast majority of tenant farmers.

RACK RENTS AND LAND-GRABBING

The scarcity of good, arable land led to what were known as 'rack rents'. If a tenant improved the productivity of his land by, for example, digging drainage ditches, clearing stones or building walls, the landlord would re-value the rent based on the improvements, and increase the rent accordingly. There was therefore little incentive for tenants to improve their land. If they did, and refused to pay the higher rent, they could be evicted. This led to the secondary problem of 'land-grabbing' whereby willing new tenants would quickly take over the holding of an evicted farmer and pay the new rent. There was therefore a real financial incentive for landlords to regularly evict their tenants, because by doing so, the landlord could increase the rent. These twin problems were recognised and tackled head-on by the Land League, to avoid undermining the collective action and to prevent the problems of eviction from being compounded:

> [Tenants] were enjoined to discourage 'land-grabbing' with all their power. This … was, of course, the most important of all, because it was plain that famine could not be caused by high rents, unless other tenants could be found to take 'evicted' farms and pay rent for them.

Anna also pointed out that:

> English 'statesmen' almost invariably allude to the fact that whereas an English landlord frequently cannot find a tenant for a vacant farm, an Irish landlord had no lack of applicants eager for the privilege of paying him rent, as a proof that Irish tenants are in a better position than English tenants.

Land-grabbing had to be stopped. Charles Stewart Parnell realised that a tour of America, and a massive fundraising campaign, would be essential to carry the campaign forwards and in late December 1879, he sailed to New York to join his sisters and to begin a speaking and fundraising tour for the 'Irish cause'.

7

Political Awareness

On 5 January 1880, one of the most famous battles of the Land War took place in Carraroe in Connemara, in the rural west of Ireland. Women were always at the front lines in defending their family home from eviction. 'Women's resistance was expected,' wrote historian Margaret Ward, 'and there is evidence that their activities ranged from verbal insults to physical attacks on those who attempted to use the battering ram against rent defaulters.'

That morning in Carraroe, the landlord's agent was carrying over one hundred and twenty eviction notices from the bailiff. The local community was standing strong in support of the Land League, and refusing to pay what they considered to be unfair rents. They were not surprised to see that the police escort was armed with rifles and bayonets. They were making a stand and refusing to pay their rent.

The *Irish World* newspaper reported what happened next:

The women and maidens were in the thickest of the fight, carrying on their backs to the men bags filled with huge rocks, which were showered in hundreds down on the process-server and his escort.

Naturally, the constabulary was not about to take this sort of pounding without retaliation, but what happened next was to become a regular occurrence at evictions and demonstrations for the duration of what was to become known as the Land War:

The constabulary charged the crowd with fixed bayonets, drove them back a little, but the people returned to the fight, having brought with them their spades, reaping hooks and great clubs, and then the fight took regular shape.

This battle continued for two entire days, during which the community managed to confiscate one hundred and sixteen eviction notices from the bailiff. The bailiff was only able to carry out four of the planned one hundred and twenty evictions, and the battle was deemed to have been a success.

As the *Irish World* was quick to point out, to the delight of readers, and using the language of war, the women were 'fighting with stones in their stockings, as the women of Limerick once fought and routed King William's troops before their walls'.

Against this backdrop, Charles Stewart Parnell was greeted like a hero on his arrival in America. Anna, Fanny and Theodosia had only a short time with him, before he headed off on a speaking tour of the USA, which had the dual aims of raising awareness of the impending famine and the need for immediate relief, and raising funds for the Land League.

When his tour began in January 1880, Côté states that there were 'ecstatic crowds of Irish-Americans who had come to meet [Charles] with brass bands and fulsome speeches'. This great enthusiasm helped Charles to cope with what was to be a gruelling tour of sixty cities in just over two months, traversing the country by steam train and stagecoach.

Unfortunately, as Côté puts it, Charles immediately became embroiled in an 'undignified and enduring squabble concerning the relief funds recently established in Ireland', in which he laid down the gauntlet and accused the other funds (apart from Sr Mary Frances Clare) of being pro-landlord, and therefore anti-tenant. At the time of Charles' visit, there were already three other famine relief funds in existence. The first was the Marlborough Trust, set up by the Duchess of Marlborough, the wife of the then lord lieutenant of Ireland. Her fundraising activities were mainly in England, but word quickly spread to the Americas as well.

The second was the Mansion House Fund, set up by the Lord Mayor of Dublin, Edmund Dwyer Gray (1845–1888). At the time he was a member of the Home Rule League, and was also serving as a member of parliament for the constituency in Tipperary. He was also the proprietor of the *Freeman's Journal*, the *Belfast Morning News* and the *Evening Telegraph*. Although he was more interested in urban affairs such as public health and water, he was a supporter of Charles Stewart Parnell, and the Mansion House Fund was set up in response to the Land

League's call for assistance for the rural poor. Using his vast array of contacts, Gray was able to call for help in England, America and Australia.

The third fund was in more direct competition with the others, having been established by James Gordon Bennett Jr, (1841–1918) who had tried to persuade Charles to join its committee. Charles declined for a number of reasons. Bennett had a reputation as a scandalous drunkard who outraged society with his behaviour; he was a flamboyant spender who lavished huge sums of money on sport and sailing, and, probably the deciding factor for Charles, he was very much pro-landlord in his politics. As publisher of the *New York Herald*, he had previously wielded his power (and the profile of his newspaper) to fund and publicise the expedition of Henry Morton Stanley to find Dr David Livingstone in Africa, and he was happy to use this power again to vent his annoyance at this snub by Charles Stewart Parnell throughout America.

One of the main reasons Charles was trying to set up a Land League Fund was because of lack of action by the British government, who listened to the continuing reassurances of Lord Lowther, the chief secretary of Ireland, who said that the poor harvest in Ireland was no worse than the one similarly affecting England.

The squabbling over humanitarian aid began with accusations that the lord lieutenant was in fact working for the landlords by presiding over evictions on the one hand, while allowing his wife to raise funds for the evicted on the other. She was accused of only providing support to tenants who wanted to pay their rent, and was thus seen as pro-landlord.

The Bennett Fund was perceived purely as a publicity stunt for the *New York Herald* despite the fact that its founder had himself generously donated a substantial $100,000 to the fund. The Lord Mayor's Fund was also under suspicion for being managed by committees made up of landlords, which caused impoverished tenants to be reluctant to apply to them for help.

Despite all the controversy around the legitimacy and management of these funds, between them they raised over £500,000, and the money was spent just as had been intended. Charles' fears may have been unfounded, but the public scrutiny of the famine relief work meant that, perhaps for the first time, money raised to help the poor in Ireland was actually being used as it was intended. Or perhaps it was the competition to be seen to be doing the best work that ensured that the funds were well spent. Whatever the reason, donating to Ireland could no longer be seen as a high-risk activity. This certainly improved confidence among Irish-Americans and Irish-Canadians that Irish affairs were in good hands.

Although in diplomatic terms Charles' accusations against these funds were a disaster, on a fundraising level this increased scrutiny of Irish famine relief appealed to the hearts and minds of the Irish-American public, and money flooded into the Land League's coffers. This influx of money led to a new problem for the Land League as most people wished to donate to famine relief and not to land agitation. In response, a second fund was set up – the Irish National Land League Famine Relief Fund, which had a separate bank account from the League's own organisation fund.

Accusations made by the miffed Bennett in the *New York Herald* that it was the Land League who were misappropriating funds didn't help the public image of the campaign, but nor did they stem the flow of money into the Land League's coffers.

And the Land League had other problems to deal with. Charles Stewart Parnell and John Dillon were terrible correspondents. Their mail often remained unopened, and if it was opened, it often remained unanswered. Donations were frequently not acknowledged, and supporters would refuse to send more money until they knew the original had been safely received. It is ironic that while all this controversy raged about misuse of funds, the Land League's financial correspondence descended into an unmanageable tangle.

The acknowledgements that were made were often inaccurate. Because monies could be sent to the Land League's offices in Dublin, their temporary office in New York, or the various newspapers and banks that collected on their behalf, they were often mixed up and the wrong amounts would be acknowledged to the wrong people for the wrong fund. This was disastrous, as there were many people who wanted just to donate to the Famine Relief Fund, and had no interest in land agitation, and so were reluctant to make any further donations for fear it would go into the wrong account.

Anna and Fanny busied themselves behind the scenes and tried their best to sort through this tangle of paperwork and correspondence. The sisters were overwhelmed by the generosity they found in the hundreds of donations they received.

Oblivious to all this – because he did not open the letters of complaint from Anna or Fanny – Charles Stewart Parnell was continuing his tour of America with all the pomp and ceremony worthy of the grandson of great American naval hero, Rear Admiral Charles Stewart.

This dynamic young Irish leader roused the hearts and opened the purses of the Irish diaspora in America. His was a just cause and his work for the starving peasants of Ireland created a groundswell of public support. Charles was warmly received throughout the United States and Canada by individual congressmen, state governors, judges and other public representatives before appearing before Congress itself.

While he was in Toronto, Canada, in January 1880, he was first hailed as the 'Uncrowned King of Ireland', a title that would forever be associated with him and which infuriated Queen Victoria. Such was his reputation and influence that he was given the given the privilege of addressing the American House of Representatives on 7 February 1880. This was a daunting task.

Although he was comfortable addressing a large group of fellow parliamentarians, he was aware that many of the Americans would have no real grasp of the situation in Ireland apart from the conflicting reports and rhetoric in the papers. His elegant solution was to base his speech on the article that Fanny wrote describing the situation in Ireland. He knew that Fanny's article expressed the situation clearly and succinctly, because following the original publication of her article (under Charles' name), John Bright himself, after whom the 'Bright Clauses' in the first Irish Land Act of 1870 were named, made a series of suggestions to make his own clauses easier to implement.

With her brother Charles now being hailed as the Uncrowned King of Ireland, and receiving the validation of his position by being invited to address the House of Representatives, Anna truly believed that the founding of the Land League in Ireland the previous October was no less an occasion than the creation of a new government for Ireland.

This high profile beginning held the promise of greater political achievement, so it was with great regret that she later stated that this foundation had not been built upon and that ultimately 'both of Ireland's governments, unfortunately, have legislated against her and for England'. But she continued with a tribute to Ireland as a diasporic empire, which was an indirect and biting comparison between Queen Victoria and her 'uncrowned' brother Charles. The glory of the British Empire in the Victorian era was that it was said to be an empire on which the sun never set, because it quite literally encompassed the globe:

> This small, wretched country [Ireland], so absolutely in the power of her bigger neighbour, the most squalid and miserable under the sun, and the most universally despised, has kept up an independent government on voluntary revenues, receiving tribute from its empire beyond the seas, on which the sun never sets, being, in fact, the only country that has a world-

wide empire proved by the strongest test there can be, the financial test.

Her focus then shifted to the support of the Irish diaspora:

For what other country is there that could levy a voluntary tribute all over the world, or from anywhere? And paid so gladly and so unquestioningly for so many years.

With the various funds pointing fingers at each other, and an already shaky reputation for financial mismanagement, the generosity of the Irish diaspora was truly breathtaking, demonstrating their trust in the leadership of the Land League.

However, the financial and administrative affairs of Charles and the Land League in America continued in a state of disarray. Donations were still left unacknowledged and correspondence left unanswered, upsetting and annoying the hundreds of people who had responded to Charles' pleas for support for the Land League Relief Funds. Charles and John Dillon continued to ignore their correspondence, focusing on making public appearances instead.

On 24 February, a twenty-four-year old journalist, Timothy Healy, was sent to America to work as secretary to Charles and John. But by then much of the damage had already been done. It is just as well that Timothy was a journalist, because his skills were needed to counter the growing frustration, which was now being reported in the newspapers, about the appalling state of the League's administrative affairs.

Charles' tour of the United States and Canada continued nonetheless, and he resolutely ignored his correspondence and stepped up his campaigning work with renewed vigour. Côté reported that 'surrounded by his immediate family and constantly reminded of the heroic deeds of his patriotic American ancestors, he began to speak with a verve and enthusiasm seldom associated with a man of his normally careful, spare prose'.

On 8 March 1880, Charles' tour was cut short unexpectedly, when the British Prime Minister Disraeli declared that he would dissolve parliament and a new election would be called. Charles knew that this new election would be a decisive indicator of his party's chance for success. He was in Montreal, Canada, at the time, and hurried to New York to finalise some business matters before heading home. The day before he sailed back to Ireland, he established the American Irish National Land League at a meeting in New York; little detail is recorded of this event.

His sister Theodosia accompanied him on the journey back to Ireland, as she was preparing for her marriage to an English naval officer, Claude Paget, in Paris that summer.

Michael Davitt soon arrived in America to organise the newly formed American Irish National Land League. Anna Parnell spent a lot of time assisting him, working both in Davitt's office and in the Famine Relief Fund Headquarters. It is here that Davitt observed Anna's superb organisational skills and her potential leadership abilities. He soon became one of her firmest admirers and strongest supporters, and she of him.

Meanwhile back in Ireland, by the spring of 1880, the threat of famine had lifted. The work of the Land League had been, for this crisis at least, successful. Although the famine had been the catalyst for the formation of the Land League, it was not the only reason the League had been established. The underlying cause of poverty and injustice in Ireland was still the system of unfair rents and absentee landlordism, which kept the rural population on the brink of ruin. Now that the immediate famine crisis was over, these underlying problems needed to be addressed. The real work of the Land League was about to begin.

In April, the British general election was held and twenty-four Parnellite Home Rulers were returned; this was a quadrupling of the original six members in the previous general election, and spirits were high in the Home Rule Party. A further twenty Home Rulers were also elected, but these were not loyal to Parnell. From America, an exuberant Michael Davitt, delighted at this success, exhorted Charles to use the opportunity of the first day of parliament on 26 April to 'make a fierce row in the House when the session begins. Notice will be taken in America and money will start to flow to the Famine Fund again.' He helpfully included a list of American newspapers to which to send stories. Clearly, the fall-off in funds was still an issue of concern and Michael was keen to use every newsworthy opportunity to encourage renewed donations.

On 29 April, the triumphant Land League held a land conference in Dublin. The plan was to introduce a bill to parliament to suspend all evictions for rent arrears in Ireland for a period of two years. This failed miserably, and the Parnellites drafted a watered-down plan to repeal a clause of the 1870 Land Act that would have the effect of allowing a tenant to claim compensation for having been evicted for rent arrears.

In New York, Michael was also disappointed by this setback and he expressed his concerns to Anna. Anna replied to Michael that it was pointless to begin infighting and bickering, as the League would 'not have made much advance with our business if we had begun arguing'.

Côté reported that: 'It was quite clear to Anna that neither the Land League nor the farmers had quite grasped the fact that they could and must help themselves by standing firm and resisting taking farms from which others had been evicted.'

Anna also knew, following three years of 'obstruction' in the British Parliament, that slowing down the passage of legislation through the governmental processes would not prevent the government from taking more draconian action in the future.

The entire success of the Land League depended on a mass civil action in which all the tenants of Ireland would stand together and refuse to pay their rents, support each other if any of them were evicted and refuse to allow anyone to rent the resulting vacant farm. This was the political strategy of the Land League.

SORTING OUT THE FAMINE RELIEF FUND

Although funds were pouring into the League's Famine Relief Fund, there were huge delays in acknowledging donations, or requests for information. This, combined with the history of misappropriation of funds, which made people hesitant to make donations in the first place, had a doubly negative impact. Anna and Fanny were very conscious of this, and in exasperation Fanny wrote on 5 May 1880 that 'fully one hundred thousand dollars have been lost to the Land League', because infuriated donors felt insulted and chose to 'send their subscriptions in anger to any other committee, provided only that it was not the Land League'.

To hammer her point home, Fanny claimed that 'a New Orleans gentleman of great prominence told me, the New Orleans people sent the greatest bulk of the money they raised to the Mansion House Committee' instead of to the Land League.

Something had to be done to address the problem. It was no longer a question of poor administration, but of ensuring the financial survival and core funding of the Land League. Anna and Fanny, still overwhelmed by the burden of correspondence, did their best to keep up. It was with relief that they heard that Michael Davitt would be setting up a separate administrative headquarters for the American Irish National Land League.

On 28 May 1880, this new headquarters opened for business at 40 University Building, Washington Square. To Anna's surprise and disbelief, although Michael hired a janitor, he didn't feel it necessary to hire an administrator. Perhaps he wanted to keep costs down, but perhaps he also didn't quite realise the extent of the burden of maintaining the League's administrative affairs. Anna, as exasperated as Fanny, but more inclined to take direct action than to write letters of complaint, took it upon herself to try to create an administrative framework in the new office. She began dividing her time between the Famine Relief Headquarters on Park Street and Michael's offices in Washington Square.

Having survived the frantic few months of fundraising activities earlier that year, Anna was now a seasoned veteran of how to manage the relationship between the League and its supporters. The fact that she had the time to do this also began to ring warning bells. A fall off in funds, and the bad publicity caused by poor administration during those key months, meant that the remaining donors needed to be encouraged to make further donations to the cause. Anna understood the importance of maintaining a good relationship with the League's supporters.

She encouraged Michael to 'pay them all the small attentions possible, to keep them in a good humour with the Land League'. She suggested that he purchase books as thank you gifts for supporters and major donors, in the hopes that they would continue to support their work.

She also considered that it was time to start reporting back to donors, and to the press, about the work of the League and its achievements, demonstrating that the funds were well spent. She was acutely aware of the need to nurture the League's supporters, commenting that it was 'necessary to nurse our people here a good deal, if they are to continue their contributions'.

Michael listened carefully to her suggestions. He admired her grasp of politics and her practical support, and was even prepared to listen when she chastised him, which she did on occasion, for 'actions she considered inopportune and ill-advised'.

A further meeting of the Land League in Dublin on 25 June continued to criticise Charles' parliamentary party for its failure to achieve the unrealistic goal of a two-year moratorium on evictions in Ireland, and for the lesser but equally unrealistic goal of compensation for evicted tenants. It became clear that there was a gap between what the Land League expected from the parliamentary party, and what it was possible to achieve.

Meanwhile, the Famine Relief Fund of the Land League had raised the bulk of the £60,000 it would raise in total, which was considerably less than the other famine funds that had far less publicity and public support. Donations were starting to dwindle. Something needed to be done to maintain momentum, but what? Touring America was taking its toll on Charles' health, and the League needed its leader back in Ireland to soothe the growing internal dissent. At the time of their greatest strength, the Land League was in danger of coming apart.

THE FIRST MENTION OF A LADIES' LAND LEAGUE
– AUGUST 1880

In New York, the astute Fanny Parnell noted that having four competing famine funds resulted in improved fundraising and performance by all of them. The competition between the funds was to their benefit, as it increased public awareness and discussion of the issues. It was a logical step for Fanny to wonder whether competition for the Land League itself might also be a good thing. Her strategy was to plan a League comprised entirely of ladies, primarily for fundraising, and calling on the ladies of America and Ireland to support them. It would also relieve the men's Land League of the onerous burden of fundraising, banking, administration and correspondence.

Fanny spoke to Michael Davitt about this idea – most likely focusing on how it would save the Land League work, rather than about it being a way to jump-start the faltering contributions to the League's Famine Relief Funds. Davitt, knowing that Fanny was an experienced fundraiser who had worked in both Paris and America, thought it was a superb idea.

Encouraged by Michael Davitt's support for the idea of creating a complementary League for ladies, Fanny wrote a letter which was published in the *Irish World* on 12 August outlining how she thought it might work.

Fanny's idea was that groups of ladies would create their own local committees, charging a membership and attendance fee of the equivalent of one dollar per person, and the monies raised would be sent to the League's offices in Dublin and New York. These committees would then begin fundraising locally, and in this way a network of ladies would tap into the local economy and bolster the League's overall fundraising. Fanny knew from experience that locally based women's groups were an effective and inexpensive way to achieve the League's goals.

Fanny also called for the groups to demonstrate compassion and enthusiasm. This was intended to complement the men's approach of activism and mass meetings that stirred up feeling against the British. As she wrote in her poem 'Hold the Harvest', the approach of the women was to be:

> Hold your peace and hold your hands,
> not a finger on them lay, boys!
> Let the pike and rifle stand, we have found a better way, boys.

She sat back and waited for replies. There were none in August, and Fanny started to become disillusioned. At the same time Anna was becoming restless. She knew that local activism required local leadership, and that either she or Fanny would need to return to Ireland to become the voice of the women of Ireland. It was a simple decision to make. Anna found the extremes of east coast weather not to her liking, and she yearned to return home to the sylvan landscape and temperate climate of County Wicklow, while Fanny was content to administer the League's office in New York.

Anna was also keen to return to Ireland to be in the thick of things. Moreover, although she was an exceptional administrator, she longed for the outdoors, and liked nothing better than long walks in the open air, in stout walking boots and a day dress. The confines of a secretarial post were not to her liking. Anna decided to leave America and return to Ireland.

The sisters knew that the effectiveness of their work would depend on an efficient and regular exchange of information between Ireland and America, combined with excellent local intelligence and motivated teams of volunteers. This was timely, because the fundraising efforts of the Land League in America were still slow, and the sisters knew they needed a fresh strategy to motivate the donor public. A renewal of fundraising activity was particularly important at this point, because the land agitation was stepping up, and the Land League would need all the funds it could get to support tenants in need. Just as the policy of withholding rent was starting to have an effect, it looked like the financial means to sustain it were being reduced. This could spell disaster.

CHARLES AND KATHARINE O'SHEA

Charles, who was always plagued with poor health, found that the tour of America and Canada exhausted him. James Patrick Mahon (1800–1891) – known as The O'Gorman Mahon – was a close friend of Willie O'Shea. In his day he had been a brilliant and colourful barrister, parliamentarian and journalist and is quoted in Katharine O'Shea's memoir of Parnell, *The Uncrowned King of Ireland*, as saying:

> If you meet Parnell, Mrs O'Shea, be good to him. His begging expedition to America has about finished him and I don't believe he will last the session out.

Charles did not like his ill health to be pointed out to him, and Katharine outlines how he was first described to her: 'how aloof and reserved he was and how he received any inquiries as to his obviously bad health with freezing hostility that gave enquirers a ruffled sense of tactlessness'.

However, despite this slightly less than glowing character report from The O'Gorman Mahon and others, Katharine decided to make it her business to invite this influential man to her next set of dinners for the Irish Party, to help her husband Willie in his political career.

Charles proved a difficult guest to pin down, and he politely declined all of Katharine's invitations to dinner. Eventually, he accepted one invitation, but failed to appear, much to Katharine's chagrin. This made her even more determined in her mission, and when someone pointed out the obviously empty chair, she vowed that 'The uncrowned King of Ireland shall sit in that chair at the next dinner I give!' Her guests applauded Katharine's determination. The usual polite methods of letters and invitations having clearly failed their purpose, Katharine decided on a more direct approach.

She and her sister Mrs Steele drove in their carriage to the House of Commons, and sent a card in to Charles, asking that he meet them in the Palace Yard. The two sisters waited patiently.

Katharine described what happened next. 'He came out, a tall, gaunt figure and deadly pale. He looked straight at me smiling and his curiously burning eyes looked into mine and with a wondering intentness that threw into my brain the sudden thought: "This man is wonderful – and different".'

She challenged him for failing to appear at dinner and

he made his usual – and completely truthful – excuse of not keeping up with his correspondence. But he promised to attend Katharine's next dinner, as soon as he returned from his sister Theodosia's wedding in Paris.

This was the moment in time that the course of Irish history would pivot in a new direction. Married to his country, and passionately fighting for the rights of the rural poor in Ireland, Charles Stewart Parnell found himself falling helplessly in love with Katharine O'Shea, a married woman; and she with him. He was thirty-four and she was thirty-five:

> In leaning forward in the cab to say good-bye a rose I was wearing in my bodice fell out onto my skirt. He picked it up and, touching it lightly with his lips, placed it in his button-hole.

Their fate was sealed from that moment. Shortly afterwards began a long and passionate correspondence between Charles and Katharine. Whereas he neglected his ordinary post to the detriment of his political career and his fundraising activities, no letter or telegram from Katharine ever went unanswered.

He wrote his first letter to her, dated 17 July 1880, even before he had left England for his sister's wedding in Paris. He daringly wrote about:

> The powerful attractions which have been tending to seduce me from my duty towards my country in the direction of Thomas's Hotel [where Katharine was staying] on my return

[from Paris] will write to you again and ask for an opportunity
of seeing you.

He arrived late for the first political dinner and Katharine noted
that he looked 'painfully ill and white, the only life-light in his
face being given by the fathomless eyes of rich brown, varying to
the brilliance of flame'. Interestingly, given that the *raison d'être*
for dining together was to advance Willie O'Shea's political
career, all of the diners were careful to avoid 'the controversial
subject of politics'.

After dinner, the group went to the theatre, where Charles
and Katharine sat at the back of the group and spoke together.
Katharine remembers having 'a feeling of complete sympathy
and companionship with him, as though I had always known
this strange, unusual man with the thin face and pinched
nostrils'.

From that moment onwards, their intimacy increased and
they found as many opportunities as possible to be together. A
few days later, he arranged to meet Katharine from the train at
Cannon Street Station, and have lunch in the station's dining-
room. But when he looked in the dining-room, he noticed
some members of the Irish Party were already dining there.
In the first indication that he knew being seen alone with a
married woman might not be good for his political career, he
suggested that she dine alone with him upstairs in his private
sitting-room at the adjoining Cannon Street Hotel instead.
They had tea together, talking politics, until he 'lapsed into one
of those long silences of his that I was already beginning to

know were dangerous in the complete sympathy they evoked between us'.

Katharine made her excuses and left, and he followed her downstairs. The members of the Irish Party that he had been so keen to avoid earlier were there in the hallway. As a married Victorian woman, she should have been horrified at being seen leaving a man's private chambers. But instead she remarked that 'as he always did afterwards when I was with him, he ignored them absolutely'. Perhaps familiar with dalliances among other party members, the gentlemen knew better than to challenge their leader on such a delicate matter. Whether any of their number warned him to be more discreet in future is not recorded, but he would have been acutely aware of this himself.

Charles wrote to Katharine on 9 September 1880 to say that he would be home with his family in Avondale from the following day, but that:

> I may tell you also in confidence that I don't feel quite so content at the prospect of ten days' absence from London amongst the hills and valleys of Wicklow as I should have done some three months since. The cause is mysterious, but perhaps you will help me to find it, or her, on my return.

Two days later he wrote to her again, saying: 'I am still in the land of the living, notwithstanding the real difficulty of either living or being, which every moment becomes more evident, in the absence of a certain kind and fair face.' He lamented that he would be 'removed from post offices and such like consolations for broken-hearted politicians'.

Later that autumn, Charles lodged for a time with Katharine and Willie O'Shea in their house at Eltham, and stopped travelling to Ireland as frequently. He was in very poor health. As Katharine remarked 'how near death's door his exertions on behalf of the famine-stricken peasants of Ireland had brought him'.

It soon became common knowledge that Charles was lodging with Willie O'Shea, but there was no indication that anyone – other than the Irish Party members who had witnessed her leaving his rooms the previous month – suspected that there was any impropriety between Charles and Katharine.

19 SEPTEMBER 1880 – THE FIRST BOYCOTT

In an attempt to curtail the continued scourge of 'land grabbing', Charles proposed a new policy at a public meeting in Ennis on 19 September 1880 – the boycott. 'What are you to do', he asked, 'to a tenant who bids for a farm from which another tenant has been evicted?' A number of voices shouted 'Shoot him!' – which was misreported in the newspapers as evidence that Charles was trying to stir up bloody violence in rural areas.

Charles continued his speech by offering an alternative to violence. He called for 'shunning' of the land-grabber:

Shun him on the road when you meet him ... shun him in the

shop ... shun him in the fair-green and in the market-place and even in the place of worship.

Charles said that by 'isolating him from the rest of the country, as if he were a leper of old – you must show your detestation of the crime he has committed'. There would soon be an opportunity to test this innovative non-violent method of undermining landlord authority.

Late in the autumn of 1880, Captain Boycott, a land agent for Lord Erne in Mayo, refused to give the ten percent rent discount demanded by the tenants. All of the tenants on Boycott's own farm immediately downed tools and his servants walked out. Captain and Mrs Boycott were suddenly forced to run the house and the farm themselves. Mrs Boycott went to the local town to buy food because the shops refused to deliver to the farm, but the shopkeepers refused to serve her.

Cut off from all supplies, Captain Boycott called for help from the military to harvest his crops. In early November, the army dispatched men from the Royal Irish Constabulary and four hundred men and officers from the 84th Regiment. For good measure, they also sent some horseback cavalry and the hospital corps in case of injury. War correspondents arrived from England to report on this extraordinary event.

To the disappointment of the press, this first 'boycott', as it was now dubbed, passed off peacefully. However, it had the required effect: for months afterwards, landlords in the region were terrified that they too would be 'boycotted' and evictions dropped significantly for the rest of the year.

THE CHURCH'S RESPONSE

The Archbishop of Cashel, Dr Croke, visited the Vatican in November to assure the Pope that the agitation in Ireland was not part of an anti-clerical uprising. This was to be expected, because in other countries in continental Europe, popular people's movements had proven to be very dangerous to the Catholic Church, and clergy were often the first victims in an armed uprising.

Archbishop Croke reassured the Vatican that the Irish people were not becoming estranged from the Church and were not in danger of losing their faith during their struggle for land reform, because they were using political means and not military ones.

The Vatican was only slightly reassured by his assertions. They had read too many reports of outrages committed in the Irish countryside, and received too many letters from angry anti-Land League Catholics in England and Ireland. This concern in the Church was to remain simmering in the background throughout the Land War.

BURNING AN EFFIGY OF ANNA PARNELL

In London, on 5 November, there was the usual breathless talk of 'gunpowder, treason and plot' and that evening Katharine was having dinner at home with Charles when she heard a rowdy commotion directly outside her house. She asked her maid what was going on.

Her maid replied: 'The procession, ma'am, have got Miss Anna Parnell in an effigy 'long-side of the Pope and was waiting outside for us to see before they burned 'em in the village.'

At first, Charles seemed unmoved by this information, and the maid left. Katharine reported that Charles then burst into a 'sudden bubble of laughter' and remarked: 'Poor Anna! Her pride in being burnt, as a menace to England, would be so drowned in horror at her company, that it would put the fire out!'

Charles was probably correct. Anna would have been delighted to know she was considered such a threat to England that the working classes were prepared to burn an effigy of her like Guy Fawkes. The burning may have been prompted by the recent media coverage of a squabble in the Vatican between two Irish priests about Anna and her ladies. But the irony was that Anna, like Charles, was not Catholic, and therefore burning an effigy of Anna alongside one of the Pope simply showed how little the public, and indeed the government, in England really understood of the true political situation in Ireland.

In any event, neither Charles nor Katharine bothered to venture outside to disperse the crowd who remained 'cheering and hooting' for some time, and eventually the crowd headed off and burned the effigies in the village, though, as Katharine pointed out 'with less amusement than they had anticipated'.

AGITATION IN NEW YORK

On 8 November, the day before Michael Davitt was due to return to Ireland, the American Ladies' Land League organised a large public meeting, to be held in the Cooper Union building, between Fourth and Fifth Avenues in New York. The Cooper Union building could seat 3,000 in the main hall.

To the surprise of many and the delight of the ladies, the hall was filled to bursting, and Côté reports that 'the dense crowds overflowed into the gas-lit halls'. The crowd comprised an almost equal mix of men and women, each of whom had paid the twenty-five cent entry fee. The guest of honour was Michael Davitt, who by then was as well known as Charles Stewart Parnell. The *Irish World* reported 'for the first time in the history of any nation in the world that an organisation composed entirely of women came to the front to do battle for the right of their mother country'.

Chaired by William E. Robinson, a local congressman, the meeting kicked off after a brief introduction with a rousing speech from Michael Davitt. The speakers were met with rapturous applause. Davitt began by putting the landlord-tenant problem into context. He talked about the confiscation of Irish lands centuries before under Oliver Cromwell and the system of Planters, and how Ireland had now become a nation with hundreds of absentee landlords, who took the rents and gave nothing back. He was also careful to clarify the reports in many newspapers about 'outrages' in Ireland. Many of these outrages, Davitt pointed out, were nothing to do with the work of the Land League, but the newspapers were intent on attributing land agitation to every criminal act.

Also, Davitt explained that many local disputes were being solved using what was called 'peasant law': the traditions and customs that had been used for hundreds of years to resolve disputes. These traditional dispute resolution mechanisms usually involved the payment of money or goods similar to the earlier Brehon laws which were now outlawed. Unfortunately, there were some particularly vicious punishments reported in the press. These included 'carding', which meant removing an offender's clothing and painfully scraping their skin with the metal comb usually used for carding wool, and 'cattle-houghing', which meant cruelly cutting the offender's animals' hamstrings to make them go lame.

The Land League did not approve of any of this and Davitt was keen to point out that these acts of brutality were not committed at the request of the Land League, nor were they a sign of a rejection of British law or a descent into anarchy. However, despite this, there was general suspicion in the English press that the Land League was behind every incident.

On 3 November, William Forster, Ireland's chief secretary, decided to prosecute Charles and the leaders of the Land League for causing dissent across Ireland. The leaders were not taken into custody, as the legal principle of Habeas Corpus stated that they could not be imprisoned without trial. Charles, who had been anticipating legal action, wrote to Katharine the following day, saying that 'the thunderbolt, as you will have seen, has at last fallen and we are in the midst of loyal preparations of a most appalling character'.

On 15 November 1880, a week after the first meeting of the American Ladies' Land League, a complementary fund-raising agency, the Ladies' Irish National Land League was formed in New York with the aim of raising money for Irish independence. The first committee comprised Mrs Delia Parnell as president, Fanny Parnell and Ellen Ford as vice-presidents, and Jane Byrne as secretary, all of whom were based in America, apart from Delia who rarely stayed in any one country for long. The choice of Mrs Delia Parnell as president was a natural and logical one because she was the daughter of Rear Admiral Charles Stewart, still remembered as the naval hero who vanquished the British ships the *Levant* and the *Cyane* sixty-five years previously with his superb seamanship. Mrs Delia Parnell was a figurehead who gave hope to those who supported the League.

DECEMBER 1880

By December 1880, both Charles and Katharine knew that the government was aware he was spending a lot of time in Eltham with her. Although he avoided taking the train, so that he would not be seen at the station too often, and entered Katharine's house through the conservatory or her sitting-room window, the government had employed detectives, who watched his comings and goings. The couple knew that they were being watched, but their passion was so strong they continued to see each other.

At one point in the year, Charles had been suffering with ill health and stayed in Katharine's house for a fortnight, in a room that the staff in the house presumed was empty. Here she gave him *Alice in Wonderland* to read and cooked him meals away from the prying eyes of her servants. She always took good care of him.

On Tuesday 28 December 1880, for the first time, Charles addressed Katharine as 'My Dearest Wife' in a letter he wrote while staying in Morrisson's hotel in Dublin. Although much of the letter was about his impending trial, he finished it by saying: 'I was immensely relieved by your letter this morning. You must take great care of yourself for my sake and your and my future.'

And even on New Year's Eve, he wrote to her about how worried he was about her health and again saying that Katharine 'must take great care of herself for the sake of our future'.

8

The Birth of the
Ladies' Land League

The fight was to save the homes of Ireland – the sacred, domestic
domain of woman's moral superiority in civilised society.

Michael Davitt, *The Fall of Feudalism in Ireland*

Women of Ireland, you must do your duty whilst your
countrymen do theirs … You cannot prevent evictions, but you
can and must prevent them from becoming massacre.

Anna Parnell, *The Boston Pilot, 26 February 1881*

By January 1881, the Land War in Ireland was truly underway.
The British government was planning to introduce a 'coercion
bill' as an emergency measure to stop the Land League. This bill
would abolish trial by jury and was threatening to imprison the
entire leadership of the League. Charles Stewart Parnell was
concerned for the well-being of his executive committee. It was
important that they avoid drawing attention to themselves as
individuals and retained a collective front.

However, there was soon to be an incident that sparked a fierce debate. Michael Davitt – who described himself as a 'Fenian, Catholic and Land-Leaguer' – had been honoured at a meeting of the Orange Lodge in County Armagh: the local grand master took the chair and endorsed the principles of the Land League. The meeting even went as far as to endorse the Land League itself. Michael was then 'chaired' at the end of the meeting – an ordeal of 'popular approval'. When he heard of this, and the outrage it caused in Dublin Castle and among landlords, Charles Stewart Parnell took Michael to one side and issued a calm, but grim warning: 'And now they will go for you too.'

Until this point, it seemed that everyone – including Dublin Castle – had forgotten the fact that Michael was officially still just a prisoner on parole from prison in England. His 'ticket of leave', or parole, could be withdrawn without notice. Whereas the other Land Leaguers would need to be tried and convicted under due process, Michael was already a convict. It was almost amusing that Dublin Castle had included him as a defendant in a state trial, when they already had the power to detain him. Charles and Michael knew it would be only a matter of days before the penny dropped and he would be recalled to England and put back in prison.

Meanwhile, the state trial of Parnell, Dillon, Egan, Brennan and Davitt was continuing, and on the 25 January, the jury finally reached a verdict. Charles Stewart Parnell was in the courtroom. There was a loud cheer as the foreman announced 'We are unanimous that we cannot agree', and the five men were freed. Charles left the courtroom in a hurry to catch the next boat to England, to fight the coercion bill in the House of Commons and to see his beloved Katharine.

Using his usual obstructionist techniques, Charles was able to keep the House in session from 4 p.m. on the Tuesday until 2 p.m. the following afternoon. Katharine watched enthralled from the ladies' gallery as her lover indulged in his favourite kind of political fight.

On 26 January 1881, Charles cabled the *Irish World* newspaper in New York that:

> Although arrests continue, the Irish people remain undaunted and unintimidated. Their perfect discipline is worth of all admiration. Money flows into the Land League, which the people now regard as their sole resource.

His cable continued:

> But, thanks to our American countrymen, the Land League has such reserve resources that, in spite of temporary coercive laws, there is no fear of the future.

In a chilling interpretation of the influx of troops into Ireland he stated a belief that 'the government hope by pouring in troops and by their arbitrary conduct in Ireland so to exasperate the people as to provoke rebellion and then to shoot down by the thousands the unarmed people'.

He finished this rather worrying report with the reassurance to the readership that the Land League was taking a more rational approach. 'As we stand at present,' he wrote, 'passive resistance to unjust laws is the stronger weapon in our hands.' The following day, Charles was back in the House of Commons to debate the coercion bill again, and kept the exhausted House in session for forty-one continuous hours.

A new element of the Land League's programme of passive resistance took shape at the meeting of the Land League executive, which was also held on 27 January 1881. It seemed inevitable that they would be arrested again and this time so would all the other leaders. They were backed into a corner. They had a plan to call a general rent strike in Ireland the day that the dreaded coercion bill was signed by Queen Victoria, and also that the entire Irish Party would stand up as one and leave the House together if it were to be passed into law. But something more was needed.

'England's back was up and Mr Forster would be driven to the adoption of the most extreme measures,' wrote Michael Davitt afterwards. 'The landlords would glut their vengeance in wholesale evictions, and there would either be state of anarchy or a tame submission of the country to the forces of coercion. This was the outlook.'

It was at this point that Michael proposed forming a Ladies' Land League in Ireland. The reaction of the other gentlemen at the meeting, including Charles, John Dillon and Thomas Brennan, was extraordinary. 'This suggestion was laughed at ... and vehemently opposed', Davitt wrote, on the grounds that establishing a league of ladies 'would invite public ridicule in appearing to put women forward in places of danger'.

But Michael persisted. 'No better allies than women could be found for such a task,' he claimed. 'They are, in certain emergencies, more dangerous to despotism [tyranny] than men. They have more courage, through having less scruples [reluctance caused by doubt], when and where their better instincts are appealed to by a militant and just cause in a fight against a mean foe.'

Michael pointed out that this was a 'fight to save the homes of Ireland', and that the enemy was the system of landlordism and evictions 'which had ruined tens of thousands of Irish girls, morally and otherwise, in evictions and in consequent misery and wrong'.

The meeting turned to a discussion about what would happen if the women were arrested as well, and Michael asked the group to imagine 'the effect this would have on the public opinion of the United States and the world if fifty or a hundred respectable young women were sent to jail as "criminals" without trial or conviction, by England's rulers in Ireland.' He also said that Anna Parnell had been consulted about the plan, 'and thoroughly approved of it'. Everyone knew of Anna's abilities, and they were in no doubt that she would be the perfect leader of this new Ladies' Land League.

Michael described the purpose of the Ladies' Land League. They would:

- Support evicted tenants
- Discourage land-grabbing
- Provide wooden dwelling huts near the evicted family's

land (for shelter and to keep a watchful eye on the vacant farm)
- Support families if any of their number was imprisoned
- Provide food for those who were imprisoned

Anna had received a letter from Charles telling her that a Ladies' Land League would be established in Dublin, but she received it the same day as the meeting. She rushed to Dublin. The men were supremely confident that their plans would work. Michael claimed that there were over a thousand branches of the Land League around the world, some of which had a thousand members, and that by February 1881 there would be an estimated one million members.

By the time Anna Parnell arrived in Dublin, the meeting was over and she was informed of her new role, much to her great surprise. With her usual speed to act, she called the first public meeting of the Ladies' Provisional Central Committee of the Irish National Land League, at the main League's head office at 39 Upper Sackville Street (later known as Upper O'Connell Street) in Dublin on 31 January 1881.

Anna chaired the meeting, and assembled a committee from those present, to create a slightly less wordy Central Land League of the Ladies of Ireland, later abbreviated to the Ladies' Land League.

Mrs Anne Deane was elected president, Mrs Kate Molony and Miss Ellen O'Leary were appointed joint treasurers, and Miss Anna Parnell, Miss Claire Stritch, Miss Nannie Lynch and Miss Harriet Byrne became honorary secretaries. These seven officers were joined by six ordinary members to form an executive committee. The six members were Mrs J.E. Jenny, Miss Beatrice Walsh, Mrs E.M. Judge, Mrs J. Byrne, Miss Virginia Lynch and another Miss Byrne. The three Miss Lynches who served on the executive (Hannah at a later date) were all sisters from a family of Fenian sympathisers. Virginia and Nannie Lynch worked with Anna in Dublin, while their sister Hannah worked in London.

Anna had created a dynamic team of young ladies, and Côté reported that 'their youth, good looks and zest for the work they were engaged in' drew many admirers. Côté reported that 'needless to say, a certain amount of mild flirting went on as young MPs and Land Leaguers dropped into the Ladies' Land League offices' and that sometimes a gentleman might occasionally be caught out in the act of letting his gaze 'rest absently on some particularly pretty girl'. Anna's Ladies were already creating quite a stir.

Unfortunately, five days later, having returned from a brief visit to London to try to persuade Charles Stewart Parnell of the merits of the all-out rent strike devised by the 'extreme wing' of the Land League, Michael Davitt was arrested. He was held briefly in Dublin Castle, before being sent back to Bow Street Court in London. Firstly the magistrate confirmed Michael Davitt's identity and then bluntly informed him: 'You are sent back to penal servitude.' When Michael asked why, the magistrate replied: 'That is no business of mine.'

Michael was grateful to find that he was not to be sent back to the harsh conditions of Dartmoor, but to Portland Prison instead. He lamented that: 'the exciting world of Irish politics would know me no more for five years – if the whole of the sentence was to be completed.'

This was a big blow to the newly formed Ladies' Land League, and to Anna Parnell personally. She and Michael had worked closely together in Ireland and America, and were in strong agreement about Irish politics. Anna believed, as did Michael, that a total rent strike at the earliest opportunity was the only way to win the Land War. In this way, she found herself aligned with what was known as the 'extreme wing' of the League.

On behalf of the Executive Committee of the Ladies' Land League, Anna wrote a heartfelt letter to the press that was later published in *The Boston Pilot* on 26 February 1881:

> Women of Ireland, you must do your duty whilst your country-men do theirs. They do not shrink from danger, and one of the noblest, Michael Davitt, has already been re-consigned to a convict cell. Be ready at least to help the evicted sufferers in every part of Ireland. You cannot prevent evictions, but you can and must prevent them from becoming massacres. Form yourselves into branches of the Ladies' Irish National Land League. Be ready to give information of evictions in your districts, to give advice and encouragement to the unhappy victims, to collect funds, and to apply those which may be entrusted to you, as emergencies arise.

The letter was signed by the honorary secretaries of the executive council of the Ladies' Land League – Anna Parnell, Claire Stritch, Nannie Lynch and Harriet Byrne.

CHARLES' AFFAIR DEEPENS

During this political upheaval and conflict, Charles Stewart Parnell sought refuge in the arms of Katharine O'Shea. He travelled frequently on the arduous journey by carriage, steam ship and train to and from Avondale and Eltham to see her as often as he could. Anna was completely unaware of Charles' affair with Katharine, and thought nothing of his haste to return to London. As the leader of the Irish Party, that is where he should be, and she most likely praised his attention to duty.

In Eltham, however, things were getting rocky. Captain William O'Shea, Katharine's husband, was becoming suspicious. Captain O'Shea arrived at Eltham unexpectedly, but fortunately Charles was not there. He accused her of hiring detectives to watch him at his lodgings in Charles Street, Haymarket. Although Katharine would later allude to her own husband's infidelities in her memoir, she denied hiring the detectives. A flaming row ensued. Katharine later wrote in her memoir that it transpired that one of Willie's friends was living in the same building, and that it was the friend's wife who had hired the detectives. Clearly, this suspicious wife did not like what the detective discovered, because she subsequently divorced him.

Captain O'Shea was jealous. Katharine said that 'flying rumours had perhaps reached his ears; and now it was too late, for he dared not formulate them, they were too vague; too late, for I had been swept into the avalanche of Parnell's love; too late, for I possessed the husband of my heart for all eternity.'

Although Charles was not in the house, some of his belongings were, in a portmanteau. Captain O'Shea found it and immediately had it removed from his house and sent to London. Katharine was deeply worried, because Captain O'Shea said he would 'challenge Parnell to fight a duel and would shoot him'.

He did indeed go to London and challenge Charles, who declined. Katharine's sister intervened and explained to Willie that Katharine was in fact a messenger between the government and the Land League. Captain O'Shea begrudgingly accepted this and spoke no more of a duel. However, he forbade Charles from staying with Katharine at Eltham. From that day onward, Katharine and Charles considered themselves a couple. 'Parnell and I were one, without further scruple without fear and without remorse.'

Charles was partial to white roses, and regularly wore one in his buttonhole. Katharine grew the flowers especially for him in her greenhouse. Charles wore them when he was in the House of Commons, and would give the rose a 'lingering touch' to let her know he knew she was observing him from the ladies' gallery. They developed a secret code for communicating. Charles would wave his handkerchief in the House to indicate where they would meet later – one signal meant Charing Cross, a different wave meant another of their meeting places. They would meet to discuss politics, or personal matters, or for him to receive replies from Katharine to the secret messages he sent through her to William Gladstone. This secret correspondence was an attempt to achieve Home Rule by means of direct personal communication with the Prime Minister.

While the male executive were discussing troop movements, rebellion, mass evictions, coercion laws, arrests and 'a kind of civil war', the Ladies' Land League were taking a calmer approach, although the press often used excited language to describe their work.

At the first meeting of the executive of the Ladies' Land League in February, they prepared a letter to issue to their fellow countrywomen. The letter exhorted the Ladies to take swift action to relieve distress, and emphasised the urgency of their work. They also knew that the presence of members of the Ladies' Land League and the local press at evictions was absolutely necessary to avoid the violent confrontations, which were widespread around Ireland. 'You cannot prevent the evictions,' said the statement, 'but you can and must prevent them from becoming massacres.'

The *Irish World* described Anna at her first public meeting in Claremorris, County Mayo on 13 February 1881, as 'burning with patriotic fervour, a tongue of forked lightning, a very Joan of Arc is she'. The subtitle for the article read 'Ireland's Women Aroused and At Work. Anna Parnell in the Field, Sounding the Keynote of the New Movement Against Landlordism: Relief not Charity the Motto.'

One of the philosophies behind having a Ladies' Land League was so that their work would be complementary to the men's. Anna said that 'while the men fight about orange and green, the ladies do their work in peace'. The Ladies' Land League therefore adopted white as their official colour. And at Anna's first public meeting in Claremorris, there was a white banner across the front of the platform, which read in gold letters 'Miss Parnell to the rescue'. She said in her speech, which was reported verbatim in the *Irish World* that their mission was 'to relieve the evicted families, and that is the really difficult thing to do – that will tax all your brains because you will have to provide them with shelter and food as well. In order to carry out this object, you will require organisation. Now, the women of Ireland have never been organised before.'

Anna reminded everyone that the male leadership was likely to be arrested like Michael Davitt and be imprisoned for some time 'so you must learn to depend on yourselves. You will have to keep a sharp eye on the landlords (laughter) and you will have to know, and tell us in Dublin, when the landlords have evicted a family, and you will have to tell us who is going to evict a family … and you will have to be very energetic about it, so that no one shall be left to want, even for a single day.'

The nascent Ladies' Land League soon found itself with even bigger problems. Rather than being given clear instructions and guidance in what to do – the tidy list Michael Davitt had described earlier – the Ladies were left to work out what they should do by themselves:

> We were supposed to be instructed in our work by the Land League, but their assistance confined itself to showing us the minute book in which they kept an account of their meetings, and allowing us access to their branch book, where the names and addresses of the principal local officials were written and – lastly but not leastly – finding fault with everything we did.

Frustrated by this, Anna asked the male executive for guidance. She almost regretted doing that, because she received mixed messages and confused instructions, with conflicting opinions:

> What one allowed ... the other objected to, each one did not always even agree with himself at different times as to the nature of our duties. The upshot of these divided counsels, naturally, was that the only course left us was to do what we thought best ourselves, though it was some time before we left off trying, more or less, to please everybody, when the fact was that we could please nobody.

She grew increasingly frustrated with the contradiction between what the Land League said and what they actually did, and she complained that, 'I have described myself as sometimes having felt uneasy about the conduct of the Land League. My uneasiness now deepened into dismay.'

She stated her reservations like a schoolteacher would describe an unruly class of students who were not obeying the rules:

> Seeing all these grown-up men, who did not, apparently, know enough to understand that they were all individually responsible for the acts of the executive so long as they remained members of it, or even to understand that they were bound by the public resolutions passed at their own meetings, and who could find no better use for us than to quarrel with us ... was enough to make even the stoutest heart fail.

By this stage, there were bitter and frequent arguments between Anna and the leaders of the Land League about how to run the Ladies' Land League. Anna, totally unafraid to state what she felt to be the truth, would no doubt have told them in no uncertain terms exactly what they were doing wrong.

Her criticisms were not well received and the relationship between the two Leagues began to deteriorate: 'As time went on the hostility manifested towards the Ladies by the authors of their being [the Land League] increased instead of diminishing.'

Anna suggested a reason for this growing hostility, using language she would no doubt have used in their presence too:

> I think now that, added to their natural resentment at our having done what they asked us to do, they soon acquired a much stronger ground for their annoyance in the discovery that we were taking the Land League seriously.

This was the point at which Anna realised that the two Leagues could not possibly continue to work together. Their views about the work of the Land League were so different, and working conditions were so difficult that Anna suggested that the Ladies' Land League should be closed. There was no one more surprised than Anna by the response of the men to this proposal:

> The proposal was received with something like fury. Notwithstanding our unhappy inability to please them … it still required a great deal of diplomacy on our part to sever our connection with our creators without an open quarrel.

History would later write that it was Charles who wanted to put an end to the Ladies' Land League, but this exchange reveals that in fact it was she who proposed ending it, and at a much earlier stage than had previously been thought. Anna was eventually persuaded not to dissolve the Ladies' Land League, although she came to regret her decision later. She considered it a great 'blunder' to have withdrawn her threat to shut down the Ladies' Land League:

> One penalty for those who make an initial blunder of great magnitude in any matter of importance, always is that nothing done by them thereafter ever seems right … So we stayed where we were, and the long squabble went on.

The turbulent relationship between the Land League and the Ladies' Land League was set to continue, but now the Ladies were in a weaker position than before, as they had backed down from this confrontation. The Land League knew that the Ladies would continue to comply with their instructions, as all good Victorian women were expected to do.

More trouble lay ahead for Anna and her Ladies. The Ladies' Land League had scarcely been in existence for six weeks when a pastoral letter from the Archbishop of Dublin, Most Reverend Edward McCabe, was read out in over two hundred churches in his diocese on Sunday 12 March 1881.

He accused the men's Land League of 'degrading the women of Ireland' by creating the Ladies' Land League in the first place. However, his pastoral letter had the opposite effect to what he had intended. There was a huge upsurge of interest in membership of the Ladies' Land League.

The popular Archbishop of Cashel, Dr Thomas Croke, gave the Ladies his stamp of approval in a rejoinder published the following Friday – St Patrick's Day – saying that the creation of a Ladies' Land League was a very prudent idea in the circumstances, and remarking that 'His Grace will not be allowed in future, I apprehend, to use his lance so freely as he has hitherto done.'

Anna found this constant discussion of her and her Ladies' work a little frustrating. She found herself defending her actions. She visited Draperstown in Ulster and spoke to her audience of Protestant ladies:

> The Ladies' Land League must expect the enemies of the Ladies' Land League to object to the work, and the more good they did, the more they would find the enemies would attack them … they must not be surprised at that … they must not be frightened. They must … remember that the more troublesome they were to a certain class of people [landlords] the better they were performing their work, for it was intended they should be troublesome.

A RIOT IN MITCHELSTOWN

In May 1881, Anna and a group of Ladies from the Mitchelstown Ladies' Land League in Cork were called to the site of a threatened mass eviction of tenants on the estate of the Dowager Countess of Kingston. In November 1880, and again in May 1881, the tenants refused to pay their rent in accordance with the Land League's policy, and demanded a rent reduction. The countess, deeply in debt herself because of enormous mortgages on the land, refused their demand and instead issued eviction notices. Many tenants paid up, but a large number continued to withhold payment and demand a reduced rent.

The county sheriff arrived in Mitchelstown to carry out the evictions, accompanied by three hundred armed soldiers and police. They found themselves face to face with 15,000 people, who threw rocks at them. The confrontation quickly deteriorated into a riot and forty people were injured. The evictions were temporarily called off.

But this temporary stay was brief and by the end of June there were around seven hundred soldiers and three hundred police guarding the countess' castle. Faced with this overwhelming force, many more tenants decided it was wisest to pay their rent.

The remaining tenants in Mitchelstown were to be evicted shortly afterwards and Anna made sure to attend every eviction personally, both to offer immediate support to those evicted and to ensure that there would be witnesses to any brutality. As one eviction was completed, Anna would march to the next farm ahead of the soldiers and wait for them to arrive.

On 10 August, Anna was shocked and appalled when a policeman assaulted a man with the butt of his rifle. The man, Patrick O'Keefe, subsequently tried to have the policemen disciplined for this attack, but was unsuccessful.

Anna's energy throughout all of this astounded the reporter from the *Freeman's Journal*, who remarked that:

> She did wonders during the day, journeying across fields and ditches, running and walking alternatively for hours in a manner that excited the wonder of all and the admiration of some.

Furious at being described in this way, Anna wrote to the *Freeman's Journal* the next day. She said that she had only crossed one field and stood on one wall, and had advised young O'Keefe to ask the sheriff's men not to abuse his cattle, which is when he was struck by the butt of a rifle.

Despite what Anna describes in her *Tale* as 'excessive noise, uproar and violent language' and the huge legal costs this campaign had incurred, most of the two hundred people who were evicted had paid their rent by the end of the day and were back in their homes. Only the twenty poorest who did not have the money to pay their rent remained homeless. And by harvest time, even these remaining few had managed to pay their rents.

Anna could see first-hand the futility of the policy of 'Rent at the Point of the Bayonet'. She saw that the people who did not pay their rent – those who were supposedly following the Land League's leadership – were simply too poor to pay their rent in the first place.

Whereas the Land League wanted the Irish peasantry to bravely refuse to pay unjust rents, this was not happening and in fact the Land League funds were being used to support the poorest of the poor. To all intents and purposes, her work was no more than an extension of the Famine Fund.

On 26 June 1881, in the middle of the eviction proceedings in Mitchelstown, the first retaliation against the Ladies' Land League occurred in the town of Kilmallock. Four of Anna's Ladies, 'the most respectable ladies of the town', were waiting by the side of the road for a lift to a meeting with Anna. They were arrested and charged with blocking the road and insulting the arresting constable. The case was listed for 8 July.

On 8 July, Anna attended court to support her four Ladies. Using her superb skills in generating publicity, Anna arranged for newspaper reporters from all over Ireland to attend as well. The courtroom was filled with dozens of respectable ladies from the local community. Anna also brought with her Jessie Craigen, a well-known trade unionist who was also a fierce campaigner for women's suffrage and a member of the English Democratic Federation.

To the great embarrassment of Major Clifford Lloyd, the resident magistrate who had ordered the arrests, the case was, quite literally, laughed out of court. The road that the four Ladies were alleged to have been blocking was seventy-five feet wide and the supposed insult was to call the arresting constable 'Major Lloyd's pet'. After this embarrassing public humiliation, there were no further attempts to arrest any of Anna's Ladies. But Anna had already begun a campaign against police brutality and this was just another example of the cruelty she had witnessed.

UNITED IRELAND

Throughout all of this time, the Land League continued to publish its regular newspaper, *United Ireland*, until, as Anna put it, 'the government began a systematic oppression of this small weekly sheet. They seized the paper in the [Ladies' Land League] office and wherever else they could find it, and imprisoned the editorial staff.'

What the government hoped would be a major blow was more of a minor inconvenience to Anna and did not prevent the Ladies from distributing the remaining copies around Ireland 'very much the same as usual'. Nor did it prevent the next issue from being written and edited, ready for publication.

'The editor of *United Ireland* continued to perform his own functions in prison,' reported Anna. She went on to remark that 'the warders much have connived in it', possibly in return for some of the delicious food that Anna was having delivered to the prison three times a day.

Anna suspected that the reason the staff of *United Ireland* were permitted to continue producing the newspaper – including writing stories, checking proofs and all the other paperwork necessary to run a newspaper – was so that the government could accuse the Land League of carrying out illegal business while in prison. But for whatever reason, this was never used against them. A slight hiccup occurred when the printers were also thrown into prison, which stopped the printing in Dublin, but Anna and her Ladies saw to it that it was printed first in England and then in France.

United Ireland was more than just an informative read; it provided welcome additional income for newspaper boys and constabulary alike. 'In Dublin, the small newspaper boys used to hide it under their uniforms of rags, and sometimes got as much as a shilling for it,' reported Anna. 'Oddly enough, the police were among the agents who helped to distribute [it], for they used to supplement their incomes by selling the copies they were able to seize, as waste paper.' And undoubtedly the waste paper merchants sold them straight back to the newspaper boys as soon as the police were gone.

Anna recognised the importance, and the humour, inherent in this little distribution scam, and the effectiveness of this small weekly newspaper in keeping hope alive across the country. 'The running of *United Ireland* was the pleasantest part of all the work of the Ladies' Land League,' reminisced Anna. 'It was something that could, at any rate, be done, and did not seem so painfully like trying to make ropes of sea sand, as so much of our other tasks did.'

While the police were watching the docks for illegally imported copies of the newspaper, 'we were taking away the illegal production concealed in our clothing and distributing it all over Ireland,' Jennie O'Toole later wrote. Billowing petticoats had many uses.

Anna recalled one incident that annoyed the government immensely. Miss Lynch, in Anna's office, had managed to print and circulate 30,000 copies of the newspaper around Ireland from their office in 32 Lower Abbey Street, under the very noses of the detectives who had cordoned off the office.

Miss Lynch was interviewed by Mr Gallagher, the editor of the *Freeman's Journal*, and shortly afterwards he blurted out: 'I hear the Ladies' Land League are going to take over *United Ireland*, but it is absurd to think a handful of girls can defy the government.' Miss Lynch wisely chose not to respond to this provocative remark, but told Anna about it later. Anna thought that since physical strength was not involved, girls could defy as well as anybody else.

On 6 July 1881, Fanny addressed a meeting of the Land League in Montreal, where she spoke again of the importance of peaceful resistance in the struggle for a reform of land rights in Ireland. 'The element of assassination should be left out of the struggle,' she pointed out, 'for it is no use trying to fight crime with crime.'

In September, Fanny became ill with a recurring fever that left her unable to get out of bed. She would seem to recover, and be quite herself again, and then suddenly have another attack. The family was worried, and it affected Fanny's ability to attend meetings and other engagements.

A SPECIAL CORRESPONDENT

A special correspondent for the *Irish World*, Henry George, arrived in Ireland in the early autumn to send first-hand accounts to his paper's eager Irish-American readership. He was hugely disappointed to discover that the Land League was focused on political action and it was in fact the Ladies' Land League that was doing all the active work. While the funds were controlled and managed from Paris by Patrick Egan, and a group of around fifteen men travelled throughout Ireland handing out grants to tenants, everything else was co-ordinated by the Ladies' Land League.

Of course, Henry dared not let his readers know this for fear of destroying American financial support for the Land League, so he focused his attention on writing articles describing brave tenants fighting for their land rights and a wicked government who was trying to oppress them.

CHARLES AND KATHARINE START A FAMILY

From the beginning of their passionate affair, Charles would travel frequently to visit Katharine. His letters show that he would often travel from Ireland just to see her for a brief meeting, before returning on the next ship. They spent every minute that they could together.

It is hardly surprising then that Katharine would discover in the autumn of 1881 that she was expecting a child – Charles' baby. The baby was due to be born in the spring of the following year. Charles was delighted, but anxious about Katharine's health, worried about being in prison during her pregnancy and upset that he could not be with her. They kept their news a secret, and no one suspected that Katharine's fourth child was not her husband's.

Katharine wrote in her memoir that on 11 October there was an arrangement between Sir Thomas Steele, the commander-in-chief of Ireland, that the arrest of Charles Stewart Parnell was to be signalled by sending a telegram with the one word: 'Proceed'.

Charles was asked one evening at dinner by an Irish MP, 'Suppose they arrest you, Mr Parnell. Have you any instructions to give us? Who will take your place?' According to Katharine's recollections, Charles replied, through a glass of champagne, 'Ah, if I am arrested Captain Moonlight will take my place.'

'Captain Moonlight' was a mysterious highwayman who terrorised the countryside of Lancashire in the 1760s. Wearing a mask, a cloak and a tricorn hat, he managed to evade escape by disappearing into the night. He was never caught and he was never seen in daylight. Legend says that he was in league with the Devil, and he delighted in setting fire to haystacks and barns.

Sure enough, on 13 October 1881, detectives arrived to arrest Charles 'on suspicion' while he was in the Morrison Hotel in Dublin. He was permitted to write one final, brief letter before they took him to Kilmainham Gaol and he chose to write to his dear Katharine:

> I have just been arrested ... the only thing that makes me worried and unhappy is that it may hurt you and our child. You know, darling, that on this account it will be wicked of you to grieve, as I can never have any other wife but you.

In London, William Gladstone was at the Guildhall and he announced that Parnell had been arrested. Katharine wrote in her memoir that Gladstone said: 'The first step has been taken in the arrest of the man who has made himself pre-eminent in the attempt to destroy the authority of the law …' From the word 'arrest', his voice was drowned out by 'the audience rising *en masse* and cheering frantically'. There was jubilation that Charles was now going to be put in prison. More arrests quickly followed, as the leadership of the Land League was systematically imprisoned: Thomas Sexton, J.J. O'Kelly, John Dillon, William O'Brien and J.P. Quinn. Moreover, warrants were issued for Joseph Biggar, Timothy Healy and Arthur O'Connor.

As the news reached Ireland, there were 'riots in Dublin' according to Katharine. 'Shops were closed,' she reported, 'and towns and villages went into mourning as if for the death of a king.'

On 14 October, Charles wrote to Katharine from Kilmainham Gaol. He was trying to reassure her that he was all right. 'I am very comfortable here,' he wrote, 'and have a beautiful room facing the sun – the best in the prison.'

He wrote later that he was happy with the company he had and was enjoying playing games with other prisoners. He also wrote to Katharine that he was able to receive his favourite periodicals: the *Times, Engineer, Engineering, Mining Journal, Pall Mall Gazette* and the *Universe*.

He further reassured her on 21 October that he was able to have his breakfast in bed and read his newspapers there too – hardly a punishment. He also wrote that he had 'quite forgotten that [he was] in prison, and should very much miss the rattle of the keys and the slam of the doors'.

His one complaint was that there were a lot of police in the gaol, and that two of them slept against his door and two under his window.

THE NO RENT MANIFESTO

Five days after Parnell's arrest, the Land League issued the No Rent Manifesto in Dublin. This document called for all the tenants of Ireland to withhold their rents with immediate effect until the prisoners were released. The manifesto itself called on tenant farmers in Ireland to 'pay no rent under any circumstances ... until the government relinquishes the existing system of terrorism and restores the constitutional rights of the people' and promising to support everyone who did so, saying that money would pour in from America to ensure that no one would suffer. Posters were distributed all over Ireland:

NO RENT! No landlords' grassland. Tenant farmers, now is the time. Now is the hour. You proved false to the first call made upon you. Redeem your character now. NO RENT until the suspects are released. The man who pays Rent (whether an abatement is offered or not) while Parnell, Dillon &c. are in Jail will be looked upon as a Traitor to his Country and a disgrace to his class. No rent, no compromise, no landlord's grassland, under any circumstances. Avoid the Police, and listen not to spying and deluding Bailiffs. No rent! Let the land thieves do their worst! The land for the people!

The lengthy manifesto was signed by all the imprisoned executive committee, including, curiously, Michael Davitt, who was in prison in England and Patrick Egan, who was in Paris at the time.

Katharine reported that, 'arrests and evictions went on all over Ireland and the Coercion Act was used mercilessly and unscrupulously on behalf of the landlords'.

Newspapers began reporting unrest in the countryside and mysterious fires at night started by person or persons unknown. Captain Moonlight, it would seem, was enthusiastically supporting the Land League.

Anna's response was less enthusiastic:

The most injudicious feature in the whole thing [No Rent Manifesto], however, was the manner in which the financial aspect of the matter was to be treated. The sentence 'Our exiled brothers in America may be relied on to contribute, if necessary, as many millions of money as they have contributed thousands', reads to me like nothing but the language of lunatics.

The Ladies' Land League and its co-ordinator, Miss Anna Parnell, became very busy indeed. As well as providing practical relief to the evicted, Anna and her Ladies were given the task of building houses for the people who were made homeless. 'The Land League, I believe,' she said, 'built some houses in the beginning, but did not continue the practice.' She was soon to find out why.

She acknowledged her own naïveté, saying that 'at starting, among other illusions, we were under the impression that houses in Ireland can be built by public enthusiasm, and the only other expenditure required being for materials, and refreshment for the enthusiasts who did the work.' A programme of building temporary homes began, but although the workers had the requisite enthusiasm, they did not have the necessary skills. One local secretary wrote to Anna, saying that:

> It [the house] is a splendid monument to the spirit of the people, but quite unfit for human habitation.

This was a problem, because Anna knew that the usual stone, mud and mortar houses took 'too long to build in time for batches of evictions'. Without somewhere to live, evicted tenants could find themselves living by the side of the road, with shelters cut into the sides of ditches, usually under a large stone or boulder, sleeping on wet straw and being utterly miserable.

Anna turned her attention to wooden houses. One builder offered to build them for £6 each, but these were just as unsatisfactory 'without even having the recommendation of testifying to the splendid spirit of the people'.

In despair, Anna turned to local builders and quickly discovered that 'we suffered from one of the inconveniences all governments are supposed to be afflicted with, in being charged higher prices than anyone else'. Eventually, the only solution was to have prefabricated houses sent from Dublin and set up where they were needed.

Anna realised at this point that the cost of providing houses would eat into her funds. But if she failed to build them, the Ladies' Land League would be accused of 'neglecting the evicted tenants and starving out the spirit of the people'. On the other hand, Anna knew that if she spent all the money, she would be accused of wasting it to build houses when it could have been used for political purposes. 'It was quite on the cards, indeed,' she said, 'that we should be blamed on each count at once.'

Since Anna knew she would be blamed for misusing money no matter what she did, she chose to spend it on helping the tenants, despite the fact that Charles had instructed her not to build any more huts for the evicted to conserve funds. 'We had no right to abandon these tenants, to whom we had incurred so much responsibility because we were ignorant of the character of the Land League heads, to please those heads when we were no longer ignorant of their character,' she wrote. 'So we disobeyed.'

The Petticoat Rebellion had begun.

IMPACT OF THE NO RENT MANIFESTO

The No Rent Manifesto was creating quite a storm across Ireland and in England, and as punishment Charles was not allowed visitors for five days. The British Government's chief secretary in Ireland – William Forster – promptly responded to the No Rent Manifesto by declaring that the Land League was now an illegal organisation. Côté reported that 'to his great surprise, the Land League obediently ceased to exist without even challenging the legality of his act'.

'The No Rent manifesto had many adherents at first. Estate after estate adopted it eagerly, on paper,' wrote Anna. But she cautioned that tenants were only adopting it because it would not affect their real intention, which was to pay their rents in full as soon as they were forced to. No one who could pay their rent really wanted to be evicted, not even to satisfy the Land League, and not for the benefit of Ireland. 'It was just as easy to say they would pay no rent as to say they would pay only so much,' continued Anna, 'when in both cases they meant to pay the whole.'

Anna knew that every tenant who could afford to pay their rent would eventually pay it in full rather than go to jail. In her mind, the No Rent Manifesto was clearly not going to work and in fact it was too late at this stage.

Meanwhile, there were reports in the newspapers of Charles' ill-health in prison, but he wrote to Katharine to say that he had pretended to be sick, in order to spend time in the infirmary consulting with other members of the Land League. Whether Katharine believed this, in light of her own personal knowledge of his ongoing poor health, is uncertain, but his letters to her spoke about how comfortable, well fed and relaxed he was.

Very soon after the No Rent Manifesto was issued, 'a doubt seemed to creep into the minds of the tenants as to the nature of the new policy', wrote Anna. It dawned on the tenants that they were taking a huge risk in following this policy and 'it occurred to them that it would be wiser to get the promise of "all costs paid by the Land League" definitely repeated, and they began to send emissaries to the office with that intent'.

Anna was deluged with requests from anxious tenants trying to confirm that the Land League would indeed honour its promises. Anna, deeply frustrated, reported that 'a perfectly awful time ensued for the Ladies'.

Because the Ladies' Land League was based in the same building as the men's Land League, 'all day we were besieged by all kinds of delegates, entreating, arguing, threatening, imploring, all with a view to extorting the desired promise, so that we literally had not time to attend to our other work', recounted Anna.

A group of tenants who rented land from one of the few genuinely wealthy landlords in Ireland – Lord Fitzwilliam – sent a representative to Anna's office to demand that the Land League give the tenants the money to buy back their farms through the county court if they were evicted for not paying rent under the No Rent Manifesto. The tenants argued that Lord Fitzwilliam was so wealthy, that there was no point in fighting him through the courts and it would be cheaper for the Land League to simply buy the land. Anna agreed that while 'it would be better for the tenants not to risk eviction if they were satisfied that they could not win', she disagreed with the principle of buying their farms in lieu of legal action for eviction, particularly because these tenants could clearly afford the rent, but were doing all of this 'for the sake of pretending they did not mean to pay'. The argument went around in circles, and eventually the tenants' representative went away, with the insight that perhaps it was best to avoid costly court proceedings and to pay the rent if they could. As Anna said:

After the noisy defiance the local leaders and the tenants had been so long engaged in lavishing on the landlords, to find themselves suddenly called on to climb down from their lofty attitude without the final display of fireworks which they had been used to look to for saving their faces must have been pretty trying, and I often felt sorry for these disappointed angry men I was compelled to send away, discontented.

Anna found these exchanges exhausting, and reported that: 'After one of these long tussles with a determined tenant, I used generally to find myself compelled to go home, too done up for any other work, and wishing tenants would only be as determined with the landlords as they were with us.'

Despite the difficulties of her day-to-day work, Anna also made sure that the prisoners in Kilmainham were well fed. Reddy Brothers provided the catering service, which was second to none. The amazing spectacle of dinner for the leaders of the Land League in the gaol was described in Hopkins' *Kilmainham Memories* pamphlet:

A long table down the centre of the hall was littered with newspapers, magazines and books of the day, draught boards, chess boards, backgammon boards and packs of cards.

The same table at the dinner-hour bore a cloth of snowy linen, was decorated with fruit, flowers and cut glass, and upheld a weight of excellent hot dishes and wines of many kinds. It might have been a succession of Horse-show weekends in Dublin, and her

Majesty's gaol at Kilmainham turned over to some enterprising caterer who had it converted for the nonce into an elegant hotel.

Anna, who co-ordinated the prisoners' menu, made sure to include cocoa, cheese, preserves, cold meats and other filling foods as appropriate for breakfast, lunch and dinner. Anna considered it important for the country to keep up the strength of the prisoners while they were in prison, and the prisoners delighted in the hearty meals she supplied.

While stories of hunger, deprivation and illness in prisons were printed in the papers, in fact the Land League leadership were enjoying a life of leisure and good food. Tasty chops were smuggled into the prison, which Charles was able to prepare himself, and he even said, contrary to the newspaper reports, 'that my health is not only as good, but better than it has been at any time for the last twelve months. I am getting all my food from the governor's kitchen and it is excellent.'

On Christmas Day, 1881, meals from the governor's kitchen were stopped, and once again Charles and the imprisoned Land Leaguers were back on prison rations.

Outside of Kilmainham, and with the failure of the house-building programme, many families were forced to live by the side of the road in makeshift dwellings. Anna provided another option. She instructed her Ladies to keep a watchful eye for forthcoming evictions, and as soon as they had news that the sheriff would be calling, they found lodgings in the nearest town for the evicted. She also instructed her Ladies to hire carts to carry the tenants' belongings with them and keep them dry. She also made a point of insisting that 'care should be taken to avoid collision with armed forces and restrain useless and irritating attacks on the military' because these would 'prevent an efficient system of relief of evicted families'.

By this stage, Anna Parnell felt being locked up in prison, rather than being a punishment for the leadership, was in fact a relaxing reward. The Ladies' Land League was working harder than ever to support the tenants of Ireland.

In addition, police would often burst into the meeting rooms of the Ladies' Land League and threaten to take down their names, or put them in jail. The incidents of intimidation grew more threatening and some of the branches started to falter. One young woman wrote to Anna despairing that none of the other members of her branch would come to meetings any more because the Royal Irish Constabulary had warned them not to. Anna replied, 'I am ashamed to hear that Irishwomen can be so cowardly.'

Anna travelled at least three times between September and December 1881 to England and Scotland, to speak to emigrant Irish people living there. The rationale for this was 'to address as many meetings in England as possible during the next few months, as it is the only way I can see open to me to put before the people of this country a portion of the real facts of the case about Ireland'.

Anna's speaking tour in England was successful, but she managed to cause controversy even there. At a meeting in

Greenock on 17 November 1881, the provost refused to bring her to the platform of the town hall because of her 'unbecoming language'. She had recently been reported as saying that William Gladstone was a 'wretched, hypocritical, bloodthirsty miscreant', which had caused outrage across England. Pro-Irish newspapers played this down, referring to her only as a 'prepossessing young lady attired in black', her signature colour.

Anna was referred to as 'a pestilent disturber' in the English press and some newspapers were also calling for her arrest. But Dublin Castle still believed that the Ladies were merely a front for the men; they couldn't comprehend that in fact Anna and her Ladies were doing all the work.

Anna knew that it was only a matter of time before the leaders of the Ladies' Land League would be imprisoned too. She had estimated that they would receive two months' grace, and her estimate was correct. In December 1881, the British government found a loophole.

The attorney general finally, and begrudgingly, conceded that in fact 'the operations of the Land League are effectively carried on through the agency of women calling themselves "Ladies" ... the Head Body in Dublin appears to superintend the organisation and their directions are carried out by the local branches'. This was all that was needed to start arresting the Ladies *en masse*.

Because the Ladies could not possibly be accused of the same coercion tactics that led to the arrest of the men in the Land League, the government chose to use an archaic piece of legislation that permitted people with a bad reputation – namely suspected prostitutes – to be imprisoned pending bail. Anna was disgusted that this old law was being used, in her view illegally, particularly since no one ever produced any evidence that any of her Ladies were of 'ill repute'. Its use was designed more to cast doubt on the morals of the Ladies themselves, and perhaps to dissuade their husbands, fathers, brothers and sons from allowing the women to continue to work. In this regard, it was an underhand, yet successful tactic. To damage the reputation of a Victorian lady was to ruin her in polite society.

Prisons were made ready to accept an influx of female prisoners. 'All preparations, even to the provision of beds for us had been made,' Anna wrote, 'when measles broke out in the prison selected for our accommodation, and caused a stay in the proceedings.' Even facing the threat of harsh prison conditions, she joked that the government probably thought, 'it would be rough on the governor to have both the measles and the Ladies' Land League on his hands at once'.

This providential outbreak of illness in prison may have caused Forster, known by the jeering nickname of 'Buckshot Forster', to reconsider his plan to arrest the Ladies' Land League *en masse*. Or perhaps he felt it would be better for his image if the Ladies were not all in prison. Whatever the reason, the Ladies and their helpers who continued delivering supplies to the poor were gradually arrested as they went about their work. Anna's network of information and communication 'became almost extinguished throughout the country'.

One woman, Hannah Reynolds, 'was imprisoned for advising a tenant not to give up possession of his holding' in December 1881. It was an unusual case, not to do with a rent strike at all, but with an argument over title of the land. If the tenant were to leave the farm, he would have lost his greater claim to the land and Hannah was correct in advising him to stay. However, she was imprisoned for a month for saying this. Fortunately, she was allowed to wear her own clothes in prison and her food was provided by the Ladies' Land League. Local bands came and played under her window, and Hannah was also allowed to receive a visitor each day.

But the clamp-down got worse and Anna reported that: 'Another girl was imprisoned for merely going to a town, where she had as much right to be as anyone else. The constabulary ordered her to leave, and on her refusing, she was sentenced to a month's imprisonment.'

Anna issued instructions to her Ladies to be cautious, to only provide shelter and support for people who were evicted, and not to give any advice at all. But even this strategy did not work. It seemed that no matter what her Ladies did, they were always imprisoned. And soon, anyone who helped the Ladies at all was arrested and put in jail too, 'even the workmen employed to erect shelters'.

Anna knew that the net was closing around them and she took the precaution to make copies of her books and records, so that if one set was confiscated, she would have another. She also reported that the women were imprisoned under harsher conditions than the men. While the men had six hours a day to exercise outside their cells, the Ladies were only allowed two, and if it rained they were not allowed out at all.

By January 1882, Anna was exhausted from organising a national relief operation from one small office in Dublin, and from being constantly asked for help. She lamented that it wasn't those Ladies who had been working the longest who were being imprisoned, but those who were new to the work. 'With one exception', Anna reported, 'only new hands were shut up, who had not been long enough at work to acquire an understanding of the delightful aspect a prison may assume under some circumstances.'

Anna laughingly reported that the 'one exception', was delighted to have the opportunity to 'seize the occasion for lying in bed of mornings, once she had a chance'. This lady so enjoyed the rest, that for the entire time of her imprisonment the governor was 'engaged in an unsuccessful attempt to get her up in proper time'. Anna herself was never arrested and eventually an order was made to release all the Ladies.

NATIONWIDE NEW YEAR'S DAY PROTEST MEETINGS

On 16 December 1881, Mr Hillier, the inspector general of the Royal Irish Constabulary, thoroughly fed up with the Ladies' Land League, issued a circular to all the offices in Ireland stating that promoting the work of the Ladies' Land League in any way and 'on any pretext by females whether under the name of the Ladies' Land League or any other designation is unlawful and criminal'.

Anna immediately called on all the branches of the Ladies' Land League to hold simultaneous meetings at 1.30 p.m. on New Year's Day 1882. She knew that this circular was illegal because 'the police cannot make laws. Only the House of Commons can do that.' But she also knew she had to challenge it immediately.

By calling all of the branches to meet at the same time, on the same day, and advertising these meetings widely in the press so that the police would be aware that they were happening, she was playing a potentially dangerous game.

The inspector general, who must have been aware of this planned rebellion against police law, could, in one afternoon, arrest the entire Ladies' Land League. It was the opportunity he had been looking for.

At 2 p.m. on New Year's Day, every branch held their meetings. Police turned up at a few of the meetings, but no arrests were made. Anna had called Hillier's bluff. He knew he had been out-manoeuvred and he backed down. As Côté said this quick thinking and strategy 'is an excellent example of the manner in which Anna's coherent set of personal and political convictions enabled her to make correct and rapid decision in a moment of crisis'.

9

Deadly Rumours

> The place of the National Land League was at once taken by
> the Ladies' Land League ... the ladies very soon outleagued
> the League.
>
> F. Hugh O'Donnell, *A History of the Irish Parliamentary Party*

While the male leaders languished in jail, Anna Parnell and
her army of dedicated ladies were still busy with their mission
to support the tenants, the evicted and the prisoners. Anna was
finding it increasingly difficult to find new Ladies to help her,
and she had no time to train them properly. Her Ladies had to
be young, strong and with understanding families willing to let
them do very heavy work. She said:

> Considerable physical strength and endurance were demanded
> by the nature of the work ... on account of the long distances
> to be traversed, the inevitable exposure to weather, and the
> very poor accommodation for travellers afforded in most parts
> of Ireland.

During the cold winter, the work was harder, dirtier and more dangerous than ever before. Her Ladies knew they risked arrest and imprisonment, as well as harassment from the local police.

A COMFORTABLE LIFE IN GAOL

The harsh outdoor life was in sharp contrast to the surprisingly comfortable conditions for the political prisoners in Kilmainham Gaol. Anna was attentive to every detail of the gentlemen's needs and was particularly careful to take care of her brother Charles' needs, given his history of ill-health. She visited him regularly; both as a caring sister and so they could meet as the leaders of the two Leagues. F. Hugh O'Donnell wrote about conditions in Kilmainham:

> It was nothing like a jail, but only a somewhat gloomy and heavily furnished apartment-house which the Government had placed at the disposal of its guests from the Land League. Barring the arbitrariness of the thing, there was little more than discomfort in having to live a few months in a healthy and semi-rural suburb of the Irish capital. 'Coercion' was absolutely ridiculous as a description of this genial parody of a Bastille. 'Supposing Forster does put the village ruffians into places like this all over Ireland,' I reflected with bitter amusement, 'how on earth does he fancy that such coercion-in-cottonwool will deter any ruffian in the country?' There must have been hundreds of thousands of Irishmen who had never been so

well housed nor so well fed in all their fives; not to mention the total absence of the lightest labour.

Charles wrote to Katharine on 7 January 1882, describing how well life in prison was still suiting him. Perhaps he wrote this simply to help reassure her during the last few weeks of her pregnancy, but for a man who was so scrupulously honest, that seems unlikely:

> I am being very well fed, chops or grilled turkey or eggs and bacon for breakfast, soup and chops for luncheon and joint and vegetables, etc., for dinner, and sometimes oysters.

He then described the procedure followed by the Ladies' Land League when a new prisoner was arrested. The prisoner was initially given the generous sum of £2, followed by fifteen shillings a week for food. This rather generous food allowance had been agreed upon with the Land League because there had been such a fuss made about the awful food at the end of 1881 and prisoners were demanding to be fed properly. This resulted in a two-fold benefit for prisoners because not only had the prison catering service improved considerably since the protests, but the fifteen shillings they received was a significant sum. Most of the prisoners opted to go back on the prison food, and either sent their weekly fifteen shillings home to their families, or saved it in a bank for their release. 'I expect the majority of the Irish people will be here after a time,' Charles joked to Katharine. 'The pay is so good and it is quite a safe place.'

He described how easy it would be to escape from jail. He reported seeing open doorways he could quickly dash through to freedom, but considered that it was better for the country if he remained inside obediently. Indeed, by 23 January he was pleased to report that he had an air gun and that he and his men were enjoying target practice every day. Kilmainham Gaol was hardly a maximum security prison.

Outside the prison walls, however, life was becoming extremely dangerous for Land League supporters and innocent bystanders. Under cover of darkness in the quiet Irish countryside, lawless bandits were committing random criminal acts designed to create fear among landlords. These bandits became personified as Captain Moonlight, but even he was not as feared as his daytime equivalent, 'the military and the Constabulary'.

These outrages were considered by the government to be the work of terrorists and a precursor to a possible armed revolution within Ireland. Newspapers in England and Ireland – although interestingly only the pro-landlord editions – were filled with stories of anarchy and wild mobs roaming the countryside. As Côté remarks, 'Angry confrontations occurred between stone-throwing peasants determined to prevent evictions and the fully armed constabulary and military accompanying bailiffs and sheriffs.'

Incidents of setting fire to hayricks were widely reported, as were incidents of shots being fired into dwellings and injuring livestock.

Rates of reported crimes rose sevenfold, although threatening letters accounted for at least half of this number, making this a surprisingly literate rabble.

Anna recalled that 'the soldiery did not, as far as I can recollect, take part in the slaughter of women and children, but the constabulary seemed, for some reason, rather to prefer attacking women and children to men.' She wrote that women and children 'were always deliberately shot at close quarters, bayoneted while lying on the ground, having fallen while running away, felled and killed with the butt end of a rifle, or in some other way slaughtered or wounded under circumstances which were incompatible with any theory of accident or confusion'.

In Anna's reckoning, the usual excuses of accidentally killing women and children because they were 'mixed up with a riotous crowd' did not apply. 'In Ireland,' she pointed out, 'no excuse is necessary.'

As well as overt criminal acts, Anna was careful to examine every request for financial help from the Ladies' Land League with great care. She knew that the Ladies were seen as a soft touch and that not all the applications were genuine. Unless evicted tenants could prove they were suffering because they were actively supporting the Land League, she had no qualms about refusing to give them any money or support, as the following letter illustrates:

Ladies' Land League, Dublin.
Sir,
In reply to the application of your branch for the relief of evicted tenants in the parishes of Ballygow and Ballyroe, I

am instructed to inform you that the records of your district having been carefully examined, no trace of manly opposition to tyranny can be detected for the past three months. Under these circumstances we are forced to doubt the reality of the distress which you ask us to alleviate. By order,

MARY GENTLE,
Secretary.[1]

It was, by now, clear to everyone that Anna Parnell and the Ladies' Land League were running a well-funded and carefully managed organisation. Even with the male Land League leaders behind bars, support for the League was as strong as ever. Virtually all crime, from theft to murder, was increasing all over Ireland. Coercion had therefore had the opposite effect of its original purpose to restore public order. But why were the Ladies not stopped? Surely it would be a simple matter to arrest Anna and her executive committee outright, rather than the piecemeal arrests that had earlier taken place, and stop the Ladies' Land League in exactly the same way as they had the gentlemen's League. But this was considered political suicide for anyone who tried to implement it.

'The Irish viceroy Lord Cowper, sadly admitted that he dared not interfere with the zealous young ladies, who were distributing Mr Egan's £80,000 among the requisite patriots of Ribbon Fenianism,' wrote F. Hugh O'Donnell, 'for fear of censure in the House of Commons.'[2]

Lord Cowper believed on a personal level that the women

should be treated 'exactly like the men', because a crime is a crime no matter what the gender of the offender. But he was afraid 'the arrest of the women would raise such as storm' that it was better to take no action. Anna became known as 'Madam Moonlight'. She was also dubbed the 'Parnellite Joan of Arc' and remained above the law.

Anna and her Ladies were now untouchable, and seemingly unstoppable. Despite occasional incidents of intimidation, 'poor Lord Cowper did not dare even to arrest the *vierges de sang* [blood virgins]'. The language describing Anna and her Ladies was becoming increasingly heroic and quasi-biblical. This worried Anna deeply, because she suspected that this new mythology around the Ladies would be used against them.

She was right. What better way to destroy a myth than to accuse these '*vierges de sang*' of immoral conduct?

A DAUGHTER FOR CHARLES AND KATHARINE

While Anna was struggling to protect the reputations of her Ladies, she remained unaware that her brother's secret paramour was heavily pregnant in England. Charles was still in prison when Katharine's daughter was born on 16 February 1882. The birth was difficult and exhausting for Katharine, but she wrote that 'the joy of possessing Parnell's child carried me through my trouble'.

The baby was called Claude Sophie O'Shea. Katharine adored her. 'She was a beautiful baby, apparently strong and healthy – for the first few weeks – and with the brown eyes of her father,' she wrote. 'This child of tragedy rarely cried, but lay watching me with eyes thoughtful and searching beyond the possibility of her little life.' Katharine observed that Claude Sophie's eyes had a 'curious gravity and understanding in them, lightened only by the little smile she gave when I came near'.

As with every young mother caring for her newborn, Katharine's day was full of the business of motherhood. She did not have as much time to write to Charles in prison and he wrote a gentle note of complaint on 5 March:

> It is so long since I have heard from you that I sometimes wonder whether you have quite forgotten me.

He wrote his complaint after a seven-day punishment in which he was not permitted to send or receive any post. This was widely misreported as 'solitary confinement' and Charles was careful to reassure Katharine that this was not the case. In any event, being unable to send post did not unduly bother Charles. 'The sentence did not trouble me much,' he wrote, 'as I am an even worse correspondent in here than I was outside.' But then he continued his letter to Katharine on a lighter note, saying 'I think you will scarcely know me when you see me again, I have become so fat.'

By the end of the month, the tone of his letters had changed. As well as continuing to reassure Katharine that he was healthy, he was deeply worried about the reports of baby Claude Sophie's ill-health.

March 27, 1882

MY OWN DARLING QUEENIE – I am very anxious about our little daughter. Is it dangerous? Was weighed yesterday – 12 st 7 lb. Have certainly gained five or six pounds since I have been here. How did Wifie find out I have grown a beard?

YOUR OWN LOVING KING
I don't think we shall be moved

Charles was struggling to bear the burden of being both political leader and absentee father. There was literally nothing he could do in either role because of his imprisonment. By this time, there were reports of a growing number of 'outrages' being reported in the newspapers. He was keen to absolve himself from any involvement in organising these and blamed the government for putting him in prison, thus leading to a lack of leadership. 'Politically it is a fortunate thing for me that I have been arrested, as the movement is breaking fast,' he wrote to Katharine.

He also assured Katharine that 'neither I nor any of my friends outside have sanctioned in any way certain recent deplorable circumstances. They are simply the result of leaving people without guidance and appear to be quite spontaneous.' He remarked that during the winter and early spring, rural labourers often had a lot of time on their hands, but that 'In any case the country is likely to quiet down as the days get longer and the crops commence to spring up.'

This clearly shows that from Charles' perspective, being in prison absolutely absolved him from any involvement in the disturbances that were going on in rural Ireland. Unfortunately, while the gentlemen's League was not being held responsible, the finger was being pointed elsewhere. Although they had a respectable front, Anna Parnell and her Ladies were perceived to be behind many of these activities and were dubbed 'Captain Moonlight in petticoats'.

COLLAPSE OF THE NO RENT MANIFESTO IN 1882

The No Rent Manifesto issued in October 1881 had failed to have the required impact. Anna and her Ladies were left with a caseload of genuine poverty cases. There were tenants who weren't withholding their rents but simply couldn't afford to pay them at all, and there were earlier eviction cases where the braver tenants had withheld their rents in the belief that the Land League would support them. This reduced the number of callers to Anna's office considerably, but, as she reported, 'they were quite enough'.

A month of so after the No Rent Manifesto was issued, both tenants and landlords slowly began to understand that the earlier policy of 'Rent at the Point of the Bayonet' 'had been dissolved into nothingness by the No Rent Manifesto' and 'a wholesale collapse of all resistance to rent ensued'. In other words, tenants stopped the pretence of withholding their rents – which were only due twice a year and therefore it was difficult to gauge within a six-month period who was actually withholding rent and who was not – and began to pay their landlords in full when 'gale day' arrived. Even some clergy began to encourage tenants to start paying their rents, and to negotiate over their arrears. The rent strike, in effect, was over and by March even Charles grudgingly acknowledged this in a letter to Katharine, 'I hear from all over the country that the tenants are everywhere settling.' The Land League had failed in its mission to bring about a full rent strike.

FATIGUE IN PRISON

By 5 April, imprisonment, fatigue, boredom, lack of exercise and the inability to take an active part in politics were taking a toll on Charles. The lack of freedom and the pain of being so far away from Katharine and their child began to eat into him, and like every human being, he wished to be free. He wrote to her in anguish:

> I love you, my darling, more and more every day and I should feel quite reconciled to giving up politics forever and living with my sweet Katie all by ourselves away from everybody and everything.

In Eltham, Katharine had other problems. Baby Claude Sophie was becoming increasingly unwell. Katharine was living in misery, caring for her sick baby. With Charles locked up in prison overseas and her husband keeping out of the way – at her request – she suffered alone. She called one doctor after another, hoping for a cure:

> I will not speak of my anguish when I found out that the child
> of my love was slowly dying and that the doctors I called in
> could do nothing for her.

Katharine was faced with the prospect of losing her child. 'Slowly she faded from me,' she wrote, 'daily gaining in that far-reaching expression that dying children have so strongly.' Watching her child die was horrendous to contemplate, but for Katharine there was something making things even worse. 'My pain was the greater in that I feared her father would never see her now.'

Baby Claude Sophie was baptised as a Catholic by Father Hart in Katharine's drawing-room, in which she had made an altar of flowers. Nothing could be done apart from wait for the inevitable.

Tragedy was soon to strike another branch of the Parnell family. In Paris, Charles' nephew Henry, his sister Delia's twenty-one year old son, died unexpectedly. Charles was given leave from prison to attend his funeral. On his way to Paris, Charles made sure to make time to travel through England and he rushed to the bedside of his dying child. 'Spring was very early that year,' wrote Katharine, 'and in the April morning when the air was fragrant with the sweet freshness of the spring flowers and the very breath of life was in the wind, Parnell came to me and I put his dying child into his arms.'

Charles was unable to stay for long; he needed to continue his journey to Paris that evening to arrive in time for the funeral. It is impossible to imagine the depth of his pain and despair.

While he was in Paris, there was an outbreak of typhoid in the American colony and 'a great many people' were affected, including his family. His sister Delia became very ill and Charles felt obliged to visit her. He knew Katharine would be worried, but he had recovered from 'ordinary typhoid' as a child and felt he was at minimal risk. Unfortunately, he caught a very bad cold and was laid up for a few days. His doctor forbade him from returning home until later in the week. Throughout this stay in Paris, he was registered at the Grand Hotel under the name of 'Stewart' and no one suspected who he was.

On Thursday 20 April 1882, Charles returned to Eltham, on the pretext of visiting Captain O'Shea to discuss the 'Irish Question' and to work on a draft text of a treaty (which eventually became known as the Kilmainham Treaty) to end the impasse between the Land League and the British government. Katharine reported that Charles and Willie sat up all night in her dining-room. 'Willie wanted me to join them,' wrote Katharine, 'but I would not leave my baby.'

As the morning sun appeared that Friday, the two men decided to rest. Charles knew he had one last thing to do before he left for Ireland. He had to see Katharine and Claude Sophie. Katharine wrote, 'My little one died as my lover stole in to kiss us both and say good-bye.' Within a few hours, Charles was forced to leave his distraught Katharine and their dead child, to return to Ireland. Baby Claude Sophie was buried in the grounds of the Catholic church at Chislehurst on 25 April. Katharine planted clematis and white roses at the foot of the granite cross.

Although Charles could not be at the funeral, he wrote Katharine a beautiful letter, lamenting that 'it is too terrible to think that on this the saddest day of all others – and, let us hope, the saddest that we both shall ever see again – my Wifie should have nobody with her'.

Shortly after the death of his first child, Charles received a visit from Captain William O'Shea in Kilmainham. He had arrived to receive the signed copy of the Kilmainham Treaty to give to Prime Minister William Gladstone. Côté summarises the Treaty perfectly, saying it was:

> … an informal agreement that [Charles Stewart] Parnell would accept the Land Act and end the campaign [of non-payment of rent] in return for an amendment to extend the fair rent clauses to leaseholders, measures to protect tenants with heavy arrears of rent and, of course, the release of the prisoners.

Captain O'Shea felt honoured to deliver this important document to the prime minister and Gladstone on his part was relieved to finally receive it. The Kilmainham Treaty was a way out of an impossible deadlock. With a rising bill for accommodating almost a thousand prisoners in jail without trial, including some members of parliament, Gladstone was struggling to find a way out of the mess without losing face. The Kilmainham Treaty was the perfect solution.

Charles also wrote a letter to Mr Gladstone on 28 April, saying that he would 'cooperate cordially' with him in future negotiations. This, at last, satisfied Mr Gladstone, who was keen to avoid another session of Irish obstructionism in parliament. The release of the Land Leaguers was imminent.

In April 1882, rumours started to spread that the current Lord Lieutenant, Francis Thomas de Grey Cowper, 7th Earl Cowper, who had only been in office since May 1880, was going to resign. The reason for his resignation was even more surprising. Anna heard the rumour that 'his reason for resignation was disgust at the kind of government he had observed in Ireland'. She didn't believe this for a minute, suggesting instead that:

> No one could hold a post which involved conniving with all that was done by the Irish government during those two years and have a scrap of conscience or a grain of scruple left at the end.

A second rumour then spread, that Mr Forster was also going to resign:

> Nobody went so far as to accuse Mr Forster of conscientious motives, but a very alarming idea seemed to spring up in the country that Mr Forster's departure would mean the end of the reign of terror, and that the English government had repented of its ways and was going to be good forthwith.

Despite how it appeared, this was not good news. Anna was instantly on the alert for what was to follow: 'And very soon a situation was to arise that required to be dealt with very ably, and was dealt with almost as wrongly as was possible.' Anna braced herself.

Lord Cowper was succeeded on 4 May 1882 by John Poyntz Spencer, 5th Earl Spencer, who had previously served as lord lieutenant from 1868 to 1874. Shortly after came the public recognition of Anna's work, which was ultimately to be its death knell: 'Now came the apotheosis of the Ladies' Land League. Cowper and Forster, it was argued, must have felt themselves beaten, or they would not have resigned, and obviously the victory must be due to the Ladies Land League. That Cowper and Forster had not been beaten ought to have been quite plain to everybody. It certainly was so to us, and we felt this brief period of fictitious triumph to be even more unsatisfactory than that cold atmosphere of censure we had so long been used to.' Anna and her Ladies were being revered as the secret power behind the Land League. It was made public that it was she and her lieutenants who were doing all the work, and this meant humiliation for the imprisoned men. Anna knew that she had been out-manoeuvred by the British government.

This simple acknowledgement of the real influence of the Ladies' Land League was enough to bring the entire Land War to an end. The male leadership was simultaneously humiliated as the Ladies were placed in personal danger. No longer could the men hide behind the Ladies' petticoats. The Petticoat Rebellion had been found out and nothing now could prevent its inevitable demise. In the eyes of the male leadership, the Ladies' Land League had to be stopped. And the only people in a position to do it were the men's Land League. More specifically, because of Anna Parnell's position and influence, the only person who could bring an end to the Ladies' Land League was Charles Stewart Parnell himself.

Anna and Charles were in the difficult position of trying to decide which of them would emerge as victor. And Anna knew it could not be her.

For the sake of Ireland, she had to back down. For the sake of the future of Irish governance, and her brother's reputation and career, she had to back down. Anna knew the only remaining question was when, and how, she would be made the sacrificial lamb. She packed her bags, and awaited imprisonment.

In April 1882, Miss Anne Kirke was arrested in Tulla for the 'crime' of overseeing the building of huts for a large number of evicted tenants. She was sentenced to three months in prison. Anna was furious. Even as she and her Ladies were facing the end of their work, they were still being harassed by the constabulary.

On 2 May 1882, the three MPs – Charles Stewart Parnell, John Dillon and J.J. O'Kelly – were released from Kilmainham Gaol by agreement of the British cabinet. Forster resigned immediately in protest. Côté continues: 'Charles arrived in the House of Commons the following day and announced that the settlement of arrears would have an enormous effect on the establishment of law and order in Ireland. The press began to write in glowing terms of the new era of conciliation.' These arrears would be settled by the setting of fair rents, the writing off of some portion of arrears and the halting of planned evictions.

Anna was relieved to hear that her brother was released from prison, remarking that:

> The end of our long nightmare was in sight. If the Land League came out of prison, they could have no excuse for leaving the work they had put on our shoulders much longer.

But she was also deeply apprehensive about what was taking place in the political arena. She had deep reservations about what this 'new era of "reconciliation", which we were being gravely assured had already commenced, was likely to bring forth' because she, and the Ladies' Land League had, as usual, been kept completely in the dark about the entire reconciliation process.

Anna considered the release-and-conciliation strategy between the Land League and the British government to be nothing less than a real-life retelling of 'The Emperor's New Clothes'. She wrote in her *Tale:*

> The situation, indeed, resembled nothing so much as that described in Hans Andersen's story of the two false tailors, who reaped much profit by pretending to make clothes with a magnificent fabric which had the magic property of being invisible to the stupid and the base.

She remarked that the government hadn't changed at all, 'unless perhaps they were getting a little worse'. She was surprised by the public reaction to all this discussion of conciliation. The most ardent critics of the government had overnight become its most enthusiastic supporters. Anna wrote: 'The government of Ireland had been clearly recognised as one of sheer persecution, with no redeeming features, by the same people who were now suddenly unable to see anything amiss with it.'

On 6 May 1882, Michael Davitt was released from Portland Prison and Charles went to Weymouth to meet him. Newspapers reported that in the village of Ballina on the previous day, a boys' band had decided to march in the streets in celebration of Davitt's release, in defiance of a ban by the constabulary. In her *Tale*, Anna explains at great length why the ban was in place. When her brother Charles had been released from prison, most houses in Ballina put a celebratory candle in the window and there was rejoicing in the streets. 'These rejoicings,' Anna pointed out, 'extended themselves to breaking the windows of some householders who failed to illuminate.' This didn't bother the householders, who were able to claim compensation through the courts. However, she pointed out, the constabulary 'were in a savage mood' because of this overt demonstration of popular support for Charles and his party. It was as if the chief constable and Mr Forster took the release of these political prisoners 'as personal slights on themselves'.

When the police heard that there would be another celebration for the release of Michael Davitt, they were furious. 'They forbade the Ballina town band to play on this occasion, on the grounds that the band had caused the aforesaid breakage of glass.' This, thought Anna, was ridiculous. She considered that 'to forbid illumination would have seemed the most direct way to save the windows of Ballina; for if nobody had illuminated, no windows would have acquired an unpopular distinction.' Anna thought that the people who had lit up their windows when her brother had been released were, 'on the face of it, more guilty in the matter of the broken windows than the band'. Nonetheless, the town band was afraid to play, 'foreseeing death', and stayed at home.

'But a children's band, from Ardnaree', wrote Anna, 'still counting on a remnant of manliness amongst these fiends in whose power they were placed, came into town to play and soon found out their mistake.'

The townsfolk listened to the children's band as they played. It was a peaceful event, until a constable 'wrested the drum away from the small drummer'. The little boy burst into tears and ran home to his mother. As Anna later recalled: 'He probably saved his life by taking this course.'

The crowd suspected that the boy's drum was likely to be destroyed:

> It is common practice with the Constabulary to break up the instruments of these local bands, and therefore the children, and everybody present, had every reason to believe the drum, once seized, was gone forever.

Some of the spectators grew angry, and 'demanded the return of the drum'. This was not going to happen and so some of the crowd began to throw stones, 'not at windows, but at the Constabulary'.

Having 'secured the pretext they wanted', Anna wrote that the police 'soon send a volley of buckshot, not at the men, but into the boys' band'. She said that 'with two exceptions, all the wounded were under fifteen, which is an additional proof that the children were deliberately aimed at'.

In normal circumstances where a riot was suspected, police would read the 'riot act', asking the crowd to disperse. 'It must be borne in mind that the Riot Act is not read in Ireland before firing on a crowd, except on rare occasions,' pointed out Anna. 'It would of course, be ridiculous to read the Riot Act to a band of children; to shoot them like mad dogs is the only course that appeals to English common sense.'

Anna wrote with sadness that one of the injured boys subsequently died. Another had been pronounced as having 'no hope of recovery', but his ultimate fate was not recorded.

THE PHOENIX PARK MURDERS

Four days after the triumphant release of Charles and the other Land League prisoners, and on the day Michael Davitt was released, the Land League was rocked by the news of a shocking double murder in Dublin. Anna wrote in her *Tale* that on the evening of 6 May 1882, 'we received news that Lord Frederick Cavendish, the new secretary to the Lord Lieutenant, and [Thomas Henry] Burke, the under secretary, who was the permanent head of the Irish government, had been killed in broad daylight in the Phoenix Park'. Both men were stabbed just outside the Vice-Regal Lodge, by a group of men later identified as members of the 'Irish Invincibles'. This shocking crime caused outrage in the public press and amongst the clergy. Fingers were pointed at the leaders of the Land League.

Michael Davitt, with the assistance of some key Land Leaguers, wrote a manifesto decrying the murders in language described by Anna in her *Tale* as 'wrongly chosen, unsuitable language' that was 'especially queer':

> On the eve of what seemed a bright future for our country [the release of the prisoners] that evil destiny which has apparently pursued us for centuries has struck another blow at our hopes which cannot be exaggerated in its disastrous consequences …
> In this hour of sorrowful gloom we venture to give an expression of our profoundest sympathy with the people of Ireland in the calamity which has befallen our cause through a horrible deed, and with those who had determined at the last hour that a policy of conciliation should supplant that of terrorism and national distrust.

Charles personally offered to resign because of the murders, but his resignation was not accepted by Gladstone; accepting it would have suggested that the Land League was behind these deaths, and this could have undermined all the political work for land reform. Michael Davitt was worried that these murders would spark a flame of revolution across Ireland, and would lead to bloody confrontation. And of course the threat of a new arrears bill to evict more tenants hung over the entire land reform movement. Anna commented in her *Tale*:

> Greatorex [a witness] had actually seen the murders done, thinking that he was only looking at a drunken squabble, and had gone straight to the spot, when he saw the two men who had been knocked down were not getting up again … When Mr Maguire [another witness, a cyclist, who had gone to the nearest police station to get help] reached the scene of the murders again, the guards from the Viceregal Lodge were putting the bodies on stretchers. How came it that the authority which had dispatched the guards had not sent for a doctor first?

Anna believed that Burke was the intended victim. 'Burke had been in office about 20 years,' she wrote in her *Tale*, 'thus Burke must have been the person aimed at, and though he might have had plenty of private enemies, the likelihood of so many combining to kill him in broad daylight for private motives was too small to be taken into consideration … The only theory left was that Burke had fallen a prey to the hatred prevailing against him all over Ireland.' Lord Cavendish, according to Anna, was just an unfortunate bystander.

In any event, the murders overshadowed and stole the glory of the victory of the recent release of the leaders of the Land League.

As soon as was feasible after the release of Charles, John Dillon and J.J. O'Kelly, and in the aftermath of the appalling crime of the Phoenix Park murders, Anna organised a meeting between them and the executive committee of the Ladies' League in 'a private house'. At first, it was an ordinary meeting, updating Charles and his colleagues about the work of the Ladies' Land League. But as the meeting came to a conclusion, Anna changed the subject. 'Before they left,' she said, 'we warned them that we wished to dissolve without unnecessary delay.' The Ladies waited for a reply from Charles.

Charles skilfully wrong-footed Anna by claiming he had no idea why the Ladies would want to dissolve their own league. Anna was caught completely off-guard. To her mind, it was blatantly obvious why they would want to stop their endless, exhausting and thankless work. She wryly remarked, 'we had overlooked the fact that their possessing this knowledge need not prevent them from pretending not to have it.'

Caught unawares, Anna blurted out two answers: first that they 'wanted rest, which was true, though not the whole truth', and second that 'it was morally impossible for [them] to go on working with the men'. Afterwards, she reflected that although it was closer to the truth, 'it hardly sounded emphatic enough'. For once, Anna had been lost for the right words.

Regardless, Charles pointed out to Anna that the Ladies' Land League could not dissolve immediately and must continue its work 'for the present'. Conscious of her caseload of needy prisoners and tenants threatened with eviction, Anna knew she had to keep working, at least for a while. In the circumstances, Anna felt she had no choice but to consent to Charles' logical humanitarian request, 'for we could not expect relief immediately'. Anna was hopeful that the gentlemen's League would soon be back on its feet.

It is important to note that the Ladies' Land League had no direct funding of its own, and depended entirely on bank transfers from the main Land League account. This was a clever preventative measure to avoid having monies being confiscated by the government. Anna wrote that: 'It was the custom of the Land League to keep both its bank accounts overdrawn – its own, and ours when it began to supply us with money. The funds had been removed to Paris, early in 1881, for safety.' When the account reached a certain level of overdraft, funds would be released to cover the deficit from the main Land League account. The bank tolerated this state of affairs, as the overdrafts continued to be honoured. Therefore, while the Ladies' Land League account was usually overdrawn, this was a political decision and not an indication of financial difficulties. All this was to change when the leaders of the Land League were released from prison, because they saw no need to continue to fund the Ladies Land League, as the Land War was effectively over.

During the time that the men were in prison, Patrick Egan in Paris had provided all the monies needed by Anna and the League. She provided a final account of all Ladies' Land League expenditure to Michael Davitt, which amounted to just over £69,372 5s 10d.

Shortly after he was released, Charles was once again keen to find funds for 'parliamentary purposes' and asked Anna not to build temporary shelters for seventy families evicted from the estate of Lord Cloncurry, in Murroe, County Limerick, although she could give them grants to spend themselves. A very stormy exchange between brother and sister followed.

Anna was livid. She said that since the withdrawal of the No Rent Manifesto, the situation of the Ladies 'became more difficult than ever'. This was because 'evictions were going on merrily, both of poverty cases and the other kind'. She added that, 'some of the latter refused to settle or return to their homes, even when we advised them to'.

Anna knew that supporting seventy evicted families would ultimately cost a lot more money than building shelters: 'if seventy families have no roof over them, much money may be spent on them without their seeming any better off for it', she commented. 'Houses, on the contrary … might be expected to act as a permanent sign and symbol that all power did not lie with the foreign enemy in possession of the country.'

Anna was also annoyed with Charles and 'told the Land League that if they wanted the houses refused, they must refuse themselves'. By this time, Anna had completely lost faith in the Land League: 'we did not, in truth, believe they would have the courage to do what they commanded us to do. In any case, we did not approve of the division of labour that left all the promising to them and all the refusing to us to do.'

And so Anna went ahead and built the shelters anyway, both for practical and political reasons, much to Charles' annoyance.

ANGER AND SUSPICION GROWS BETWEEN THE
LADIES AND THE GENTLEMEN

The conflict between grassroots action and political advocacy had been a cause of disagreement between Anna and Charles since the very beginning, and now Anna's act of defiance in building the shelters proved to be the final straw for Charles. On top of this personal anger with his sister, Charles was becoming 'wary of the Ladies, for he suspected Dillon and Davitt were planning on using the Ladies' Land League to further their own ambitions', according to Côté.

He voiced his suspicions to Katharine in a letter. 'Davitt and Dillon quarrelled with me,' he wrote, 'because I won't allow further expenditure by the Ladies.' This was, he said, because Dillon and Davitt 'were in hopes of creating a party against me in the country'.

By this stage, relations between Charles and Anna had completely broken down. She considered him to be a traitor for signing the 'Treachery of Kilmainham' and for refusing to help the evicted as he had promised. And he accused her of plotting against him with some of his best friends to usurp his political leadership.

F. Hugh O'Donnell reported later that Michael Davitt 'often related to me how furious Parnell was at the refusal of the ladies to recognise Parnell's treaty with the government as any reason for interrupting the irregular war against landlordism'. He wrote of the verbal exchange between Anna and Charles:

'I have agreed that there must be quiet in the country, and I am the judge,' Charles is reported to have said to Anna.

'But we should never have done this work,' replied Anna, 'if we did not believe that you would never, never, make terms with an English Government.'

'You have had plenty of money to cover all your trouble and expense. You shall have no more,' retorted Charles.

'But we are in debt. We have promised to pay people all over Ireland,' Anna insisted.

Charles was adamant. 'You will get no more money from me.'

Michael Davitt remarked that it was with extreme difficulty that he began negotiations with Charles to send one final cheque of £500 to the Ladies' Land League. 'They have squandered the money given to them,' Charles is alleged to have said, 'and I shall take care that they get no more.'

O'Donnell reported that Michael Davitt pushed his protest against this 'shabby treatment' of the Ladies' Land League to the point of a personal quarrel, by refusing to see Charles until he had provided enough to pay 'at least the pressing debts of the ladies'. And so one final cheque of £500 was begrudgingly sent to the Ladies' Land League.

AN ENCOUNTER WITH THE NEW LORD LIEUTENANT

One day in early June, Anna was walking along Westmoreland Street, when Earl Spencer, the new lord lieutenant of Ireland, passed by in his carriage. Anna considered Earl Spencer to be 'a crueller man than Forster'. He had been appointed to his second term as lord lieutenant shortly after the Ballina killings, 'and did not punish the criminals, thereby signifying his approval of the crime'.

Anna recognised Earl Spencer immediately, and she stepped out into the road and grabbed the horses by their head collars. The driver stopped the carriage immediately and Earl Spencer looked out to see what was happening. Anna demanded to know why he would not allow her Ladies to provide shelter for evicted tenants.

This incident was widely reported in the press as an example of Anna's outrageous (and courageous) behaviour. It was considered both extremely brave and extremely shocking for a lady. Anna, in her usual self-deprecating manner, later wrote to the *Nation* and explained in her letter published on 16 June 1882 that she had simply 'met Lord Spencer on the way to the [Dublin] Castle'.

By this time, Anna was hoping that her brother would keep to his promise to dissolve the Ladies' Land League. 'From the first week in May we had cherished hopes of an early release from a long and uncongenial bondage,' she wrote, adding that, 'as time wore on, these hopes appeared less and less likely to be fulfilled.'

In America, on 18 July 1882, Anna's sister Fanny took her usual evening walk with her two pet dogs, a St Bernard and a brown setter. She seemed in good form. The following day she collected her post from Bordentown in the morning, had lunch with her mother, and went to rest in her room.

A short time later, Delia discovered Fanny unconscious in bed. The doctor was called, and he pronounced her dead of 'paralysis of the heart'. Anna received a telegram from Bordentown with the devastating news. Her health was already suffering from the exertions of running the Ladies' Land League, and the fall-out with her brother. She was suffering 'from a series of painful and debilitating boils'.

Côté reported that:

> Anna's nature had always contained that deep strain of melancholy so often found in those who reject the comforting illusions which help their more sanguine sisters to ease the pain of living.

It was reported in the papers that Anna was 'stricken down by news of her sister's death' and she became desperately ill. In fact, Anna had secretly attempted suicide. Perhaps she used poison like her sister had tried many years previously, but the details were never made public, and Anna never referred to it in her *Tale*. 'Miss Parnell is dangerously ill with brain fever,' reported *The Times*. 'Mr Parnell has been telegraphed for.'

Even during all of this turmoil, Anna lamented that: 'No word reached us for arrangements to take over the work [of the Ladies' Land League]. May passed away, and June and July, and our noses were still at the grindstone.' By this stage Anna no longer believed that her brother would keep his earlier promise.

WHAT KATHARINE THOUGHT OF ANNA

Katharine reported that 'while in Kilmainham Parnell had found it absolutely impossible to control in any way the incitements to crime and the wild expenditure of the Ladies' Land League'. This is probably based on newspaper reports, such as the *Englishwoman's Review*, which considered the Ladies' Land League to be nothing more than 'an illegal effort by female relatives of the native Irish to pursue a cowardly fight against those who were part of the civilising mission in Ireland'. The *Review* also considered that the Ladies had 'become the tools of others and misled into committing offences'. The *Review* continued by saying that the women should be locked up as well: 'We have never desired to see women freed from the responsibility of their political or their criminal acts … Why indeed should not the Irish ladies, as well as the Irish men, be prepared to incur the same consequences for illegal acts as their husbands and brothers.'

This was echoed by the *Northern Whig* paper, which suggested that the Ladies were committing 'treason, sedition and agrarian violence' which was 'no more justifiable when carried on by women than by men'. Katharine also knew how well Charles had been fed in prison; she had seen the menus and knew that Charles had gained weight. If all the prisoners ate as well as he did, then of course the catering bills would be enormous, and this expenditure were seen as extravagant.

In her memoir, Katharine described Anna in language that thinly disguised her distaste – and begrudging admiration – for Anna's unfeminine role as commander of an army of militant

ladies. 'Anna Parnell was at the head of this marvellous organisation which she spread in well-ordered ramifications [branches]
throughout the country,' said Katharine. She compared Anna's
work to a superbly organised military operation, saying, 'Her
generalship was magnificent and complete, and there appeared
to be no detail of this revolutionary army with which she was
not completely familiar and completely determined to control.'

Katharine asserts that Charles repeatedly wrote to Anna from
prison, 'pointing out the crass folly of the criminality for which the
Ladies' League, now, solely existed'. She claimed that 'this league
of anarchy' was putting the Land League into a 'hopeless financial
situation'. Katharine claimed that Anna was recklessly spending
money that had been raised in America for Charles' work:

> The fanatical spirit in these ladies was extreme; in Anna Parnell
> it was abnormal and Parnell saw no other way of saving her, or
> the country, from her folly but by fulfilling his threat of vetoing
> the payment of another penny to the Ladies' Land League.

Katharine added that cutting off their funds 'automatically broke
up this wild army of mercenaries'. Katharine also reported that
Anna never spoke to Charles again. 'Anna Parnell never forgave
her brother for this act and to the last day of his life refused to
hold any communication with him again.'

As was usual practice, the Ladies' Land League bank account was in the red at the time when Charles was released
from prison. Shortly after his release, Anna wired to Paris for
more money, but there was no reply. She tried again on several

occasions. The requests 'were not refused,' she deduced, 'but simply ignored, and we then guessed that the Land League had now, for some reason, decided to leave the country in our hands, while keeping those hands empty'.

Applications for grants continued to arrive from desperate tenants all over Ireland. Anna continued to write cheques from the overdrawn account, in the hopes that the cheques would either be refused, in which case it was a matter for the Land League, or the cheques would continue to be honoured, which would help the poor and evicted.

Anna noted that 'the manager of the bank got frightened and came to tell us so, more than once'. Despite these pleas from a nervous banker, 'the bank, apparently, was too afraid of the Land League to take action, and the overdraft went on piling up'.

Anna knew that there would inevitably be a confrontation. And she suspected that the overdraft was not an accident, but a 'last strategic move of the Land League'. She decided at that point to keep the Ladies' own membership subscriptions to one side, because 'we foresaw that we should certainly need some ready money for our most vital necessities'. She also knew that it would be simple enough for the Ladies' Land League to wind itself up on the grounds that it had no funds, but her Ladies were against this, and Anna knew that it would be bad publicity for both the Leagues.

Throughout this time, Anna received 'constant communi-cation' from the gentlemen's League, who continued to find fault with all their work. Anna leaped on this opportunity to suggest to the men 'in properly diplomatic language', of course, 'that they should do the work themselves, since they knew how it ought to be done'. Anna tried to achieve this by asking the gentlemen to start making decisions on some of the applications for grants. 'In vain we prepared bundles of "cases" for them to exercise their wisdom on,' she wrote. 'They were only returned when sent by post, and their personal delivery was met by flight.' The gentlemen refused to accept delivery of the cases.

The overdraft was now around £5,000, an enormous sum. At this stage, the Land League met with Anna to negotiate a way out of the situation. She sat back to listen what they had to say. She could hardly believe the proposal they were making. 'Our release had never been intended to take place,' wrote Anna. 'Our creators meant to grapple us to themselves permanently with hooks of steel – at least with one hook, and the bank overdraft was to be that one.' Anna was still recovering from the death of her sister and her own suicide attempt, but her wits were as sharp as ever. She braced herself for more.

'At the beginning of August we were officially informed that the Land League would not discharge the debt to the bank unless we agreed to their terms.' In brief, all of the Ladies of the executive committee were to sign an agreement. 'The terms were that the Ladies' Land League should dissolve, and *afterwards*, were to consider all applications for grants made to the Land League and make recommendations on them.'

In other words, the executive committee of Ladies' Land League must pledge to continue their work, even after their organisation was shut down. In return for this, the Land League would pay back the Ladies' overdraft. The agreement would be binding only to the five or six Ladies who signed the agreement. Anna considered this to be 'very Irish' indeed. She considered making decisions about grants 'to be very troublesome. For us it was the most laborious and sickening of all we had to do.' It was particularly difficult to work out which cases were genuine, and of course if the Ladies' Land League were dissolved, they would have no first-hand reports about the cases, as her Ladies would no longer collect intelligence around Ireland. They would be making decisions in the dark.

Once she overcame her initial amusement at this ridiculous idea, Anna made one final, devastating point, which was probably at the heart of all the friction between the two Leagues since their beginning:

> [They] wanted us for a buffer between them and the country
> – a perpetual petticoat screen behind which they could shelter,
> not from the government, but from the people.

Anna and her Ladies absolutely refused to sign the document. 'We met it with a prompt negative,' wrote Anna. 'We told them that we would give them all the information we had, and would even give secretarial assistance for a time, but the responsibilities of what grants their policies and promises had made obligatory on the Land League, they must take on themselves. We would have none of it.'

The gentlemen left, leaving the agreement behind for the Ladies to reconsider. 'Here a deadlock ensued,' said Anna, 'for both sides held firm.'

The United Ireland newspaper reported on 12 August that:

Mr Parnell and Mr Dillon had a long interview on Monday with the executive of the Ladies' Land League in Dublin, to arrange for relieving them of the labours devolving upon them since the suppression of the Land League. It is proposed to establish an open organisation, in which the ladies will not take part.

Annoyed with the way they were being manipulated, but unable to do anything about it, the Ladies turned their attention to the problem of how to deal with their demanding workload. Anna wrote in her *Tale* that as well as being 'morally impossible', the work 'was now becoming nearly physically impossible as well'.

The head office of the Ladies' Land League was down to three people, of which Anna was one. 'Of these three,' wrote Anna, 'one was too ill to go to the office at all.' This 'one' was possibly Anna herself, whose recent suicide attempt had left her very unwell. 'The other two had been obliged to go to the seaside to recuperate,' she continued. 'The result was that the papers had begun to get into confusion.'

Anna wanted to dissolve the Ladies' Land League, but still some of her committees 'continued to shrink from it'. For many, it had been the most exciting and rewarding work of their lives, and to dissolve in disgrace was not acceptable. They wanted to find a way to finish their work with their dignity intact, and for the Land League to accept some of the blame for not providing the Ladies' League with the financial means to fulfil all of the Land League's generous promises to the tenants of Ireland.

Anna notes in her *Tale* that her committee compared the Ladies' Land League to the children of Israel, and the gentlemen's Land League to the 'hosts of the Egyptians'. They said that if the children of Israel (the Ladies) crossed the Red Sea, i.e. dissolved, then 'the hosts of the Egyptians would pursue them and the parallel would be completed by the drowning of the Egyptians'. And if that happened, her Ladies continued, 'then the children of Israel would be held responsible for the disaster'. It is clear from this that Anna and her committee considered that the destruction of the Ladies' Land League would ultimately lead to the destruction of the Land League itself – a political disaster of biblical proportions.

The deadlock seemed destined to continue, until one day Anna discovered, almost by accident, 'that the fatal vow required from us was so drafted that the alteration of one word would change its nature so completely as to remove the penal consequences intended for the signatories'. Frustratingly, Anna never recorded which particular word this was, although perhaps it could have been something as simple as typing 'not' instead of 'now': 'we do not agree' and 'we do now agree' mean two entirely different things.

Laughingly, Anna reported that 'the amazing document was copied out and, after the necessary editing, was lavishly signed by all its intended victims. It was, I heard, accepted with effusion.' She never did find out if the gentlemen had overlooked the small alteration, or whether they were just grateful that the whole ordeal was over.

Anna continued the biblical analogy:

Thus the Israelites made good their escape, and the Egyptians were not overwhelmed by the Red Sea this time.

Unable to hold back one final quip, Anna commented that 'they found their way in there later on; their character made it inevitable that they should'. At last, the Ladies had found an escape route. 'We did not allow time for grass to grow under our feet now,' wrote Anna. She gave notice of the resolution to dissolve the Ladies' Land League at the next weekly meeting in August and the resolution was carried the following week.

There was one final, brief scare, when the Ladies' treasurer reported that they still had a final few grants to be paid and not enough money. Thankfully, though, the treasurer later revised her figures and Anna was spared the embarrassment of trying to raise a final sum of £100 or £200.

Their books were finally closed in late August. Côté wrote that:

while Anna was profoundly disillusioned by the turn events had taken in Ireland … she kept her own counsel, gave no interviews and never discussed in public the circumstances under which the Ladies' Land League had come to an end.

Anna wrote in her *Tale*: 'So at length the ghost of the Ladies' Land League rested in peace.'

10

After the Dust Settles

It is in 1882 that Anna's trail goes cold, and her story reverts to fingerprints in the dust. What happened to her after the Ladies' Land League was finally laid to rest – where did she go, what did she do? How did she earn a living?

In his 2006 essay 'No Turning Back: Anna Parnell', historian Pauric Travers laments the lack of information about Anna after the death of the Ladies' Land League. He remarks that after 1882, Anna 'was dogged by personal ill-health and led a peripatetic existence, often living under an assumed name'.

Anna's mother Delia, like her own mother before her, was fond of the good life and like her sons she enjoyed speculating, which bordered on gambling. She had lost a lot of money, sometimes quite publicly and even in one instance in 1882 there had been a court case against her. In 1884, Charles purchased the Stewart family estate in Bordentown from his mother. Charles, it seems, had purchased Ironsides to ensure that his mother's home could not be used as collateral for any further borrowing. Anna visited her mother there.

Two years later, it was reported in newspapers that Delia was once again penniless. She returned to Avondale in September 1886, where she again found country life to be very dull, although she was forced to stay there because of her financial circumstances.

Anna's sister Emily was now living at Avondale with her daughter, keeping house while Charles spent much of his time at Eltham with Katharine and their two daughters, Claire and Katharine. Anna was living mostly in London and paid occasional visits to her family and friends in Ireland.

Anna had not vanished from the public eye entirely. As a strong-willed woman who had been fired with political passion, she occasionally re-emerged on the political stage. On Friday 20 November 1886, Anna addressed a crowd at 8.30 p.m. in Barkworth Road in North Camberwell in support of her friend Helen Taylor, a member of the Radical Liberals. This was a campaigning event to try and secure her friend's candidature for nomination to parliament. Camberwell, a rural retreat famed for its healing waters, was situated in the county of Surrey at the time, but later became part of the county of London.

Anna Parnell and Michael Davitt shared many close friends and political ideologies throughout the Land War. In 1886, Michael married an American, Mary Yore. They returned to Ireland for a while and stayed in the Land League cottage in Ballybrack, County Dublin, which had been given as a wedding present to Michael Davitt and his wife Mary 'by the people of Ireland' in recognition of his role in the Land League.

In 1889, Anna moved to a fishing village in Cornwall on the

south west coast of England, called Marazion, where she began painting again.

In November 1890, the scandal of her brother Charles' involvement in the divorce of Katharine O'Shea was splashed across every newspaper. Anna was horrified, both at the scandal itself and at the invasion of her brother's privacy. The story sent shockwaves throughout Victorian society; this was a respectably married Englishwoman, together with the iciest, most withdrawn Irish political leader imaginable, exposed in the gutter press as an adulterous couple. And not only that, but they had concealed their affair and already had three children together.

The scandal split the Irish Party in two when Gladstone threatened to withdraw his support for Home Rule if Charles remained as president of the party. Charles was stung into replying that achieving Home Rule didn't require Gladstone's support. Within the party itself, support became polarised into those who felt Charles should continue to lead them, and those who thought he should resign. The sixty members of parliament were permanently divided – three-quarters of them against Charles.

In addition to his political disagreements with Charles, Michael Davitt opposed Charles during this ugly, very public divorce in 1890, when many of Charles' oldest friends and colleagues abandoned him. Politically, the two men had moved too far apart, and in the House of Commons, Michael sided with the Irish National Federation, which was an anti-Parnellite group.

When Katharine and William's divorce was finalised in June

1891, Charles and Katharine married almost immediately. This too caused scandal. Across Ireland, clergy denounced him from the pulpit, saying that Catholics should not vote for him.

During this time, Charles travelled nearly every week to Ireland to try to drum up support for the party. The constant travel was beginning to take its toll, and Charles' health deteriorated.

By October, less than four months after marrying his beloved Katharine, Charles became seriously ill. He returned from Ireland to his home in the English seaside town of Brighton and died on 6 October 1891. There are many disputed accounts of his last words. Some say that on his last breath he spoke of Ireland, but Katharine insists that his last words were to her alone: 'Kiss me sweet Wifie, and I will try to sleep a little.' He gently slipped into unconsciousness while his kiss was still warm on her lips and died in her arms.

Whether Anna had prior knowledge of Charles' affair is not known. She never spoke or wrote about it publicly. However, with the publicity surrounding the affair, Anna could have easily deduced that the birth and death in 1882 of baby Claude Sophie O'Shea (Parnell), must have had an impact on Charles during his imprisonment in Kilmainham Gaol. Her arguments with Charles, the deepening rift between them, could have at last made sense to her. These were not the actions of an unreasonable parliamentarian; they were the actions of a man in deep personal distress.

Her political differences with her brother were compounded with an undoubted sense of betrayal. How could he have been willing to sacrifice so much from the comfort of a prison cell where she herself had brought him food and wine and ensured he had warm blankets and plenty of amusements, when he knew how much she and her Ladies were physically struggling in the cold Irish countryside? Perhaps we will never know.

Anna's nomadic lifestyle continued. In April 1895, she was living in the Suffolk coastal town of Southwold, where she wrote her own will.

In 1897, Delia made the long journey from Bordentown to Avondale for the last time. Bordentown was leased to an industrial training school for African-American children, and Delia, now in her eighties, had finally resigned herself to a quiet life in the Irish countryside. Sadly, a few months later, on 26 March 1898, Delia suffered a tragic accident at home. Her clothing caught fire in her bedroom, and although the fire was put out by her daughter Emily, she died the following day, from a combination of burns and shock.

Delia, although she had made some unwise investments, had made sure to bequeath a lump sum to each of her daughters so that they might invest it themselves to provide an income for life. She knew from experience that this was far preferable to the unreliable annuities which were payable from their male relatives' estates.

The Parnell family had lost a lot of money over the years in investments: quarries, speculation and mining had swallowed much of the family's wealth. Like his father before him, Charles had failed to ensure that his will made proper provision for his family, and when he died it was found to be invalid as it was made before he was married. Rather than being passed to his widow and children, the estate instead went to his delighted older brother John. Unfortunately, the estate was still carrying an enormous debt of tens of thousands of pounds. Charles' investments were continuing to lose money, and John realised that Avondale would have to be sold.

The estate was sold to a Dublin businessman in 1900, with a clause in the contract saying that John could buy it back again in two years' time. John, however, never managed to raise the money and the 1902 deadline passed. John's last chance to purchase Avondale was lost.

Anna kept in contact with Jennie Wyse Power, née O'Toole, (1858–1941), who was one of the founding members of the Ladies' Land League. Jennie was involved with Inghinidhe na hÉireann (Daughters of Ireland), which had been founded by Maud Gonne. Despite her own dire financial circumstances, Anna donated £1 to a fund for the Patriotic Children's Treat Committee. When Inghinidhe na hÉireann opposed the visit of King Edward VII to Ireland in 1903, Anna sent a telegram supporting their stance. Jennie Wyse Power went on to become a founding member of Sinn Féin.

Jennie attended a national convention on 28 November 1905, in the Rotunda in Dublin, directly opposite the old Land League headquarters. This was to be the first annual Convention of the National Council of the Sinn Féin party, which was established that day. In 1911, she was elected vice-president, having served on its executive committee from the very beginning. She was also elected first president of the women's republican group, Cumann na mBan.

Jennie had learned from her work with the Ladies' Land League that overcoming poverty required more than simply political work; it required practical grassroots initiatives as well. She influenced Sinn Féin policies to include setting up small cottage industries, a Ladies' Land League initiative which had proved very successful in Connemara.

In 1904, close to destitution because her brother John had stopped paying her annuity, Anna was stung by the publication of Michael Davitt's memoir *The Fall of Feudalism in Ireland*. While Michael considered that he had been generous in his assessment of what he considered the success of the Ladies' Land League, Anna instead felt that the entire Land War had been nothing but a great sham, with herself and her Ladies as pawns in a political game. She was particularly annoyed about the following:

> Miss Anna Parnell was a lady of remarkable ability and energy of character – fragile in form, of medium height, dark-brown hair and kindly eyes, the handsome Parnell face, with all her great bother's intense application to any one thing at a time, and with much more than even his resoluteness of purpose in any enterprise that might enlist her interest and advocacy, together with a thorough revolutionary spirit. Having been very much blamed on the one hand for suggesting the plan thus agreed upon, I am vain enough to covet the honor [*sic*] too generously given me on the other hand by Miss Parnell, in her

own too modest account of the part she had played in creating the force which pulled coercion down.

Anna's rejoinder to Davitt in a speech given on 2 April 1881 was:

> The resolutions passed here to-day describe this Ladies' Land League as being jointly my work and that of Michael Davitt. Now it was wholly his work. I did not have anything to say to it until it was done. We did not put our heads together about it. Mr Davitt settled it all in his own mind, and he then informed the world that I was going to do it, to carry his ideas out, and he never asked my consent at all. I am glad now that he did not, because I might have hesitated; but now I see that he was right, and that the Ladies' Land League was the proper thing to form in the crisis at which we have arrived. I think that certain people in Dublin Castle have the same opinion, because I observe that, of all those who have been arrested, it is the special friends of the Ladies' Land League who have been pounced upon. Michael Davitt was the first.

This spurred Anna from her melancholy. She moved from her seaside lodgings to London and began writing her rejoinder to Michael's *Fall*. She began work on her *Tale of a Great Sham*. Anna's bitterness at her sense of betrayal by the Land League, her brother, her friends and the British government poured onto the pages in a stream of consciousness that sometimes bordered on a rant and it took many years to complete.

Without a regular source of income, Anna was forced to pawn what few possessions she had left, including some of her clothes, to pay for her lodgings in London. The legacy from Delia's estate had still not been resolved. Anna had compiled a 'slim volume' of poetry in the hopes that it would be published. Grateful for having a means to secretly help her, Anna's friends paid her a fictitious advance from a publisher, as they knew she would refuse to accept charity. They found a Dublin publisher willing to assist them channel some money to her. John Dillon agreed to cover the full costs of publication, and a payment of £50 to Anna, if the publisher would write to Anna and pretend that he wanted to publish the work on its merit. The publisher agreed, and *Old Tales and New* was published in both London and Dublin in 1905, although it was not a literary or financial success.

In her poetry, Anna was vociferous in her attacks on Queen Victoria as head of state. One poem, written to mark the sixtieth anniversary of her coronation in 1897, accused the Queen of ascending to a throne that was 'all stained, by filth engrained, and the blood that cries to heaven'. Victoria was labelled by Anna as the 'famine queen' and Anna did not lament her death, but instead wrote, 'that dead form will never more be seen, in pomp of fancied glory and of pride, or humbled, scorned defeated as she died.'

Death was to become a stronger theme for Anna over the coming years. She had lived with depression for decades and having survived one suicide attempt in 1882 and one episode of suicidal depression in 1904, it is hardly surprising that her continued ill-health, her ongoing sense of betrayal, her near-destitution and her exile from her beloved Avondale extinguished much of her happiness in life.

When she was in her early fifties Anna, reflecting on how she felt about life in her late thirties, wrote the following stanza in her poem 'Middle Age' which was published in 1905:

I am longing to be gone,
Though my years are not two score,
Though my course is but half-run,
I've no wish to travel more.

Anna earned £50 in total from the sale of *Old Tales and New*. The fictitious advance from her publisher, which was in fact from her well-meaning friends, was just enough to enable her to move back to the coast in the winter of 1904.

Comfortably settled in a healthier in environment, Anna wrote a letter of complaint in May 1905 to the publishers of Michael's book *The Fall of Feudalism in Ireland*, accusing them of libel. Her letter was passed to Michael Davitt, who was surprised by her accusations, and rather worried about the prospects of being sued by Anna. However, after a brief exchange of letters, she spoke no more about libel. She ended her final letter with the comments: 'I have nothing to add to what I have already said' and asked that 'no more of Mr Davitt's impudent letters be sent on to me'.

In 1907 Anna finally completed her *Tale*, and the *Irish Peasant* newspaper printed it in instalments as a regular column during the spring and summer of that year. This newspaper did not have a wide readership and the column did not generate much interest. Anna began her long and unsuccessful efforts to find a publisher. For Anna, nothing but a solid volume which could sit alongside Michael's book on the shelves of bookshops and libraries would do. Anna felt that she had not been heard, and by now, *The Fall of Feudalism* was starting to appear on reading lists for historians. Anna knew that her story of the Ladies' Land League was in danger of being written out of history. But publishers were not interested.

A FINAL HUMILIATION

Anna supported the aims of Sinn Féin, although at that time the party was still developing, and did not have a large membership. However, Anna was never one to avoid a challenge and was not averse to fighting against the odds. In 1908, she made one of her rare visits home to Ireland, most likely at the request of Jennie Wyse-Power, to campaign for C.J. Dolan, a Sinn Féin candidate for a by-election in North Leitrim.

Unfortunately, this visit was a disaster for Anna. Her rousing speech backfired, as she called for people to vote for Dolan not because he was the best candidate, or because he was for the Sinn Féin party, but because the Irish Party were 'humbugs' and voters should elect Dolan for the sake of old times. As Pauric Travers remarks, 'unfortunately, recollection of old times was not a priority in a campaign that was nasty and rotten'.

During this contentious campaign, a public meeting was held in the village of Drumkeerin. Anna, who had travelled there to speak, was assaulted by the crowd, who threw rotten potatoes and eggs at the platform. They then poured a pail of water over her. There was uproar in the press about her public humiliation, particularly the nationalist press who claimed that she was assaulted solely 'for the wearing of the green'.

Unsurprisingly, this was the last time that Anna is reported to have appeared on the political stage. Despite her best efforts, and the massive publicity about the campaign, Dolan was defeated in the by-election.

In 1910, Anna, now in her late fifties, finally inherited £1,500 from her mother's estate. Because of careful investment by her sister Theodosia, and her customary thrift and frugality, she was able to live on the interest. Anna returned to her self-imposed exile in England, and never again returned to Ireland.

HELENA MOLONY EDITS THE *TALE*

Anna grew frustrated with her unsuccessful efforts to find a publishing company willing to produce her *Tale* in book form. More than anything, Anna wanted to set the record straight, and by this time she was willing to compromise some of her strongest sentiments to achieve this. She entrusted her loyal friend and comrade from her Ladies' Land League days, Helena Molony, with the task of editing the manuscript in the hopes that it would then attract a publisher.

While Helena was editing the manuscript, King George V paid an official royal visit to Ireland in July 1911. This visit was extremely unpopular, and there were strong campaigns opposing it. In protest, Helena threw stones at a picture of the king and was fined forty shillings. Helena refused to pay the fine, and was sentenced to a month's imprisonment. Anna paid the fine, and Helena was released from jail to complete the difficult task of editing the draft text. Unfortunately, even Helena's dedicated work was not sufficient to find a publisher.

With the regular income from her inheritance, and her financial struggles finally behind her, Anna retired to the small seaside town of Ilfracombe in Devon on the south-west coast of England, using the assumed name of Cerisa Palmer. Her landlady was the genial Mrs Rowe, and Anna was often the only lodger in her comfortable but modest house at 6 Avenue Road.

Ilfracombe was a popular Victorian seaside town with good rail access, a theatre and its own pier, and it benefited from a sheltered bathing area known as the Tunnels Baths popular with day-trippers. The summer of 1911 was particularly pleasant, and Anna, who had loved the sea since she was a little girl and who was a good swimmer, swam frequently.

She went swimming in the Tunnels Baths at lunchtime on 20 September 1911. At first, the sea was calm although the tide was turning, but a short time later, Anna was swept out of the baths and out to sea. A small group of people witnessed this, but were unable to help because the sea had become too rough; a boat was needed. By the time the boat reached Anna, it was too late.

The following day, the coroner confirmed that Anna had died from 'accidental drowning' and her true identity was revealed. None of Anna's surviving family and friends were able to attend the funeral due to age and infirmity, and the only people present were her landlady (accompanied by her sister and two friends) and the manager of the Tunnels Baths with two attendants. Anna was buried on Saturday, in the cemetery of the Holy Trinity Church in Ilfracombe.

Helena Molony, more determined than ever to honour her friend's memory, continued trying to find a publisher. Dublin Castle, however, irritated by Helena's continuing political work, sent detectives to raid her office in Westmoreland Street. None of her papers survived this raid, and it was assumed that Anna's *Tale* had been destroyed.

This setback did not prevent Helena continuing her own political work, although she must have been bitterly disappointed. Helena remained a republican activist and she was involved in the 1916 Easter Rising, including, it is rumoured, firing the first shot at Dublin Castle.

Miraculously, in 1959, a dusty parcel addressed to Helena Molony was found in a stash of papers in the house of the recently deceased Sarah Fraser. How it came to be there, no one knew. The parcel was delivered to Helena, forty years after it was originally prepared for posting. Helena was incredulous to discover that it contained Anna's lost manuscript.

She rolled up her sleeves, and once again resumed her mission to have Anna's voice heard. Unfortunately, the *Tale* still did not find a publisher. The manuscript ended up in the possession of the National Library of Ireland.

It was uncovered again by Dana Hearne in the mid 1980s, who continued Helena's mission. With the addition of a contextual analysis of the *Tale*, and some more careful editing, this revised text was finally published by Arlen House in 1986, in a small, blue hardback edition, and printed by Genprint, a Dublin-based printing company.

THE EPITAPH IS ALSO THE NEW BEGINNING

The former Ladies' Land League headquarters in Dublin is now a branch of the AIB Bank at the corner of O'Connell Street (formerly Sackville Place) and the appropriately re-named Parnell Square. It is in this building that the mysterious carved stone plaque is situated, high on a wall diagonally opposite the main door. The enigma of who affixed it there is as much a mystery as Anna Parnell herself.

Kilmainham Gaol is now a visitor centre, with guided tours available to the public. The gaol had been the unwilling home of many leading Irish historical figures from uprisings in 1798, 1803, 1848, 1867 and 1916. The seven signatories of the 1916 Poblacht na hÉireann: Pádraig Pearse, James Connolly, Thomas Clarke, Thomas MacDonagh, Seán MacDermott, Joseph Plunkett and Éamonn Ceannt were all executed by firing squad in Kilmainham in May 1916.

Avondale, the Parnell family home in Wicklow, is also a visitor centre, with a more peaceful legacy. Its fertile soil is home to Coillte Teoranta, the Irish forestry commission. Every year in August, members of the Parnell Society travel from all around the world to celebrate the life and times of the Parnell family.

In 2002, the Society travelled to Ilfracombe, and planted a beech from Avondale in memory of Anna. The president of Ireland, Her Excellency Mary McAleese, wrote a short memorial speech about the work of Anna and the Ladies' Land League, which was read out at Anna's graveside, and which is reprinted as at the start of this volume by kind permission of the Parnell Society and Áras an Uachtaráin.

Now, in the twenty-first century, we can stand at the edge of the peaceful forests of Avondale, overlooking the beautiful Avoca river. Although Anna and Charles fought on different fronts, they were fighting together for the equitable and just distribution of the land. They stood proudly alongside the farmers, the landless labourers, the tenants and the evicted, to ensure that the verdant abundance of Ireland would be shared equitably among all those who called it home.

Avondale, and the history of the Parnell family who lived there, is now the property of the people of Ireland.

Notes

Introduction

1   O'Donnell *A History of the Irish Parliamentary Party*.

2   The 'Irish Question' was a phrase commonly used in the nineteenth century by parliamentarians and the press in England to describe the puzzle of how to reconcile the issue of Irish nationalism, while retaining British rule.

3   Healy, *Letters and Leaders of my Day*.

Chapter I

1   Scurvy – A vitamin C deficiency, characterised by bleeding gums, and in the very worst cases, death.

2   Gregg, *A Social and Economic History of Britain 1760–1972*.

3   Moody & Martin, *The Course of Irish History*.

4   *Boston Pilot*, 12 December 1845.

5   *Ibid*, p.162.

6   The *Blue Books* were reports to the government by Royal Commission on the health and cleanliness of the poor, in response to increasing evidence that cholera and other 'fevers' were caused by poor hygiene. See Gregg, *A Social and Economic History of Britain 1760–1972*.

7   Chadwick, *Report on the Sanitary Condition of the Labouring Population*.

8   Malpass & Murie, *Housing Policy and Practice*.

9   Dublin, National Library of Ireland, Mounteagle, MS 13,397.

10   Gregg, *A Social and Economic History of Britain 1760–1972*.

11   de Lavergne, *Rural Economy of England, Scotland and Ireland*.

Chapter 2

1   Moody & Martin, *The Course of Irish History*.

2   Côté, *Fanny & Anna Parnell, Ireland's Patriot Sisters*.

3   In the nineteenth century, fathers were automatically the guardians of the children. When John died without making Delia the guardian, it was up to the executors of his will to decide who would have custody, but when they failed to act Delia had to obtain guardianship by making them Wards of the Court.

4   Kimmel, *The Gendered Society*.

5   *Ibid*.

6   The 'Trent Affair' (aka the 'Mason and Slidell Affair'), when the British mail ship the *Trent* was captured by the USS *San Jacinto* and two Confederate diplomats found on board were taken prisoner by the Lincoln administration. Britain was furious that a Royal Mail vessel should be interfered with in such a manner, and the Confederates hoped that this would lead to a severing of the good relations between the Lincoln administration and Britain. The argument escalated to such a level that war seemed inevitable, but after the intercession of Prince Albert, the Lincoln administration released the two prisoners (although without issuing an apology) and international relations were restored.

Chapter 3

1   *Boston Pilot*, 26 February 1881 – Anna talks of 'that great Western Republic [America] where millions of our race have been exiled and scattered', indicating how she sees herself as Irish.

2   Evans mentioned them in his volume about the American Ambulance, *History of the American Ambulance established in Paris during the Siege of 1870-71* (London 1873).

Chapter 4

1   Hill, *Homes for the London Poor*.

2 Schneller, *Anna Parnell's Political Journalism*.

3 The South Africa Bill proposed the establishment of a union of South African colonies and states, but was never passed, and ultimately political unrest in the area led to the first Boer War (1880-81).

Chapter 5

1 Tarn, *Five Per Cent Philanthropy*.

Chapter 6

1 This refers to Davitt, Daly and Killen who were so called for an allegedly inflammatory speech Davitt had given at Gurteen, County Sligo.

2 The 'Bright Clauses' were drafted by social reformer John Bright to permit Irish tenants to borrow mortgage loans from the British government for two-thirds of the cost, at a 5 per cent fixed rate of interest over thirty-five years, but only if the landlord was willing to sell. This had limited success, because few tenants could raise the one-third deposit, and fewer landlords were willing to sell their profitable holdings.

Chapter 9

1 Taken from F. Hugh O'Donnell.

2 The lord lieutenant of Ireland was also commonly referred to as the viceroy.

Bibliography

Chadwick, E., *Report on the Sanitary Condition of the Labouring Population* (London 1842)

Côté, Jane McL., *Fanny & Anna Parnell, Ireland's Patriot Sisters* (Macmillan Academic and Professional Limited, London 1991)

Davitt, Michael, *The Fall of Feudalism in Ireland: Or the Story of the Land League Revolution* (Harper and Brothers, 1904)

Dublin, National Library of Ireland, Mounteagle, MS 13,397; edited in Noel Kissane. *The Irish Famine: a documentary history* (Dublin 1995)

Gregg, Pauline, *A Social and Economic History of Britain 1760-1972*, seventh edition (Harrap, London 1973)

Healy, T.M., *Letters and Leaders of my Day* (London 1929)

Hill, Octavia, *Homes of the London Poor* (Macmillan, London 1875)

Hill, Octavia, *Our Common Land* (Macmillan, London 1877)

Kimmel, Michael, *The Gendered Society* (OUP USA, 2nd Edition, 2004)

de Lavergne, Léonce, *Rural Economy of England, Scotland and Ireland* (Edinburgh 1855)

Malpass, Peter & Murie, Alan, *Housing Policy and Practice*, (2nd Edition, Macmillan Education, 1987)

McCartney, Donal & Travers, Pauric, *The Ivy Leaf, The Parnells Remembered* (University College Dublin Press, Dublin 2006)

Moody, T.W. & Martin, F.X., *The Course of Irish History* (revised & enlarged edition, Mercier Press in association with Radio Telefís Éireann, Dublin 2001)

O'Donnell, F. Hugh, *A History of the Irish Parliamentary Party* (Longmans Green, London 1910)

Parnell, Anna, *The Tale of a Great Sham*, edited by Dana Hearne (Arlen House, Dublin 1986)

Power, Anne, *Hovels to High Rise, State Housing in Europe since 1850* (Routledge Press, London 1993)

Schneller, Beverly E., *Anna Parnell's Political Journalism: A Critical Edition (Irish Research Studies)* (Academica Press, 2001)

Tarn, J.N., *Five Per Cent Philanthropy* (Cambridge University Press, 1973)

Journals & Periodicals

Boston Pilot (1881)
Celtic Monthly, The (May to July 1880)
North American Review (1879)
United Ireland (distributed by the Ladies Land League, 1881–1882)